Y0-BZM-141

THE STORY OF
YOUR FAVORITE MEAL

THE STORY OF YOUR FAVORITE MEAL

HOW TO LISTEN TO YOUR FOOD

LAURA ISHAM

NEW DEGREE PRESS

COPYRIGHT © 2020 LAURA ISHAM

All rights reserved.

THE STORY OF YOUR FAVORITE MEAL

How to Listen to Your Food

ISBN   978-1-64137-953-3   *Paperback*

978-1-64137-769-0   *Kindle Ebook*

978-1-64137-770-6   *Ebook*

I dedicate this to my parents, Sally and John, for their support of this process, including sending emails about food and enabling the procrastination with phone calls and FaceTime, which brought me much joy.

Also, to my husband, Davis, for adding in his two (or more) cents when asked for it.

And to Munchkin for being my companion during late nights of writing and for being such a good guard kitty.

CONTENTS

———

INTRODUCTION

———

We can choose to simply react to our environment or we can make the conscious decision to act with direction, purpose, and in search of fulfillment. You become the creator of situations, instead of the reactor. You become the cause, instead of the effect.

—GILLIAN MCKEITH, PHD; NUTRITIONIST,
AUTHOR, GENUINE BAD ASS

What if you had the ability to pursue your every interest to the utmost extent, without the constraints of time or limited energy? In the 1998 movie *Sliding Doors,* the main character, Helen (played by Gwyneth Paltrow), hurrying down the stairs to the subway platform, is forced to move around a child walking up the stairs and just misses her train.[1] Her action immediately rewinds. The scene starts again, but this time, the parent pulls the child out of her way, and she just makes it onto her train, beginning her parallel life to that

———

1   Peter Howitt, *Sliding Doors,* (1998; Los Angeles, CA: Miramax Films, Intermedia Films, Mirage Enterprises, Paramount Pictures), film.

of the previous scene. At times it is frustrating that Helen is completely unaware of her two different realities. But she is able to explore multiple different passions—something I have often envied.

There's not enough time in life to accomplish everything I want to accomplish. I have wished for that magic of what happened to Helen to happen in real life, enabling me to lead two separate lives or pursue multiple fulfilling careers. In all fairness, I would want to be aware of the separate realities because of the sense of fulfillment (and control). But, frankly, why couldn't I have done it all? Why couldn't I have gone to graduate school for physical therapy *and* completed culinary school *and* educated myself about food *and* surrounded myself with creative food innovators *and* written a book about it?

Funny story—I did find a way to do just that, mostly. Life doesn't have to be led in a perfectly straight line. I may never have the abilities of a movie character, but with a little self-help from authors like Jen Sincero, action happens. You see, I was inspired from recently reading (twice) *You are a Badass* by Sincero.[2] She talks about getting your butt in gear, and whatever it is, whatever you want to be doing, you simply put it out to the universe.

So, with this book I am putting my passion for food out into the universe.

---

2   Jen Sincero, *You are a Badass: How to Stop Doubting Your Greatness and Start Living an Awesome Life* (Philadelphia: Running Press, 2013), 47.

I believe these are important topics to be discussed, and I'm hoping this book can create a discussion around tastier, healthful, more sustainable meal choices. My version of healthy may not jive with yours, which is okay. I'm going to teach you how to listen to your food through sharing my process and some stories from the people who have inspired me. My goal is for you to be more informed, while curious, about understanding how to make each component on your plate taste its best (hint: something about soil and seasons).

I'd venture to say not everybody has the ability—or interest—to work on a farm or in a kitchen. But like you, I am invested in learning where my food comes from and how to make better choices to leave less of a footprint on the planet and support my region's food system. So, I'm going to start by bringing these pieces together and make this information more accessible to everyone. Think of this as a self-help book for the curious, conscious eater. I am here to help you listen to your food's story so you can learn about its journey and how that impacts your life.

We have the ability to look at the favorite meal on our plate and know exactly where it comes from. Isn't that powerful? Perhaps you have already mapped out the story of your roasted chicken's travels: backward from your plate, to the kitchen, to the van, to the crate, to the package, to slaughter, to living on the farm. If you haven't, let's do it together.

I know I want my meals to be tasty, healthful, accessible, and made of easy-to-assemble ingredients. I want to support sustainable practices without it being fancy or stressful. I believe many people feel this way, and I want you to know your food choices can be the best for yourself, your food region, and the world.

YOUR FAVORITE MEAL IS TALKING—HOW TO LISTEN TO ITS STORY

If you listen very closely, your favorite meal is telling you a story—one that it wants you to know in order for you to understand where it came from. Whether you are eating your mother's cheesy garlic bread or your favorite seasonal stew in wintertime, it's been on a journey, just like all of us.

I was personally inclined to assume that a single piece of cauliflower doesn't have a particularly complicated backstory. But a stew with many different vegetables, perhaps made with beef stock and ethically raised beef, does sound complicated. Even a single carrot in that stew has a unique story unto itself. It can be overwhelming to consider all the different facets of the question, "Where did this food come from, and how was it grown?" I personally wanted to understand how to find these stories behind everything I eat so I could make healthier choices (not just physiologically) for my life.

I have struggled with choosing healthy, and I know healthy can be tasty. Yet I usually love the art of making food more than the act of eating it. But this isn't a cookbook! So, knowing the importance of the journey of the carrot in the stew, I needed to find the storytellers, AKA experts.

Someone who greatly inspired this process is New York chef Dan Barber. Chef Barber and his team work at the farm, agricultural center, and education hub Stone Barns Center for

Food and Agriculture in Westchester, New York. Stone Barns provides the backdrop for many collaborations between Barber and other international food producers who want to produce clean, delicious food. He has done three major things to help me understand the journey of a favorite meal:

1. With Row 7 Seed Company, he is creating a grassroots movement (pun intended) to produce ingredients from seeds grown organically on US soil, stating, "The best ingredients start before they are grown."[3] Somewhat like David v. Goliath, with Goliath being Bayer.
2. With his vegetable breeder, he breeds for flavor instead of yield which shows me that through different iterations and cross pollination, something like a butternut squash transforms into a smaller, more delicious version of itself.
3. He's told stories on stage and in print about farmers of everything from wheat to fish to foie gras, focusing on environmental sustainability and ethical treatment of animals.

Following his lead, I have realized there is an accessible way in which I too can share our food's stories: through writing. He, like the other storytellers mentioned in this book, discusses the benefits of taking a step back and really looking at what you're eating. Whether you come from a background of poor choices or want to have a lifestyle filled with more interesting ingredients, this book will be your guide. I look forward to sharing with you and helping you along the way.

---

3   "Our Story," Row 7 Seed Company, accessed May 18, 2020.

THE COMPLEXITIES OF THE SYSTEM

Having picked up this book, just like the ditty about your roasted chicken's journey, you might already have an idea of how complex our food system is. We will discuss more of these details throughout the book to expose the fact that we can feel a little out of control with so many options, which complicates matters. What we do have control over is the choices we make with what resources we have. Therefore, I want you to be aware of how the food system has changed within the last one hundred years. Isn't it strange to grab and go from a vending machine or order via conveyer belt? Or even to see images of larger, faster farming equipment even though hundreds of millions of people worldwide are hungry.[4]

A connection should be made.

For instance, in developed countries, we are exposed to monstrous stores where we are inundated with choices of multiple brands and varieties of everything year-round due to upgraded technology for refrigeration, preservation, and genetic modifications. This phenomenon is even evident in the name "supermarket." You can find anything and everything year-round. What's wrong with that, you ask? I bet if you were to ask a five-year-old where milk comes from, they'd say, "From the supermarket."

Aside from year-round produce, for some, the dilemma of buying conventionally versus organically grown produce is at the forefront of food shopping overwhelm. This is not

---

4   "Hunger Map 2019," World Food Programme, August 14, 2019.

only complicated but also controversial, especially when you add the option of "local." I also understand not everyone has access to, nor can afford to buy, organically grown foods. Nor do they want to support the carbon emissions of shipping the organic blueberries from Peru when you can talk to your local farmer who might not have the money to support a full certification but can promise they do not use any synthetic fertilizers or pesticides. The system clearly doesn't prioritize buying from the friendly farmer at the outdoor stand.

It becomes controversial when acknowledging a) the country of origin is employing people year-round, oftentimes women, to support the world's demand for out-of-season produce, and b) there is no label to state how the produce arrived in your country.[5] It might leave more of a carbon footprint to drive a gas-guzzler to your local market to buy the local blueberries in June. And there has been great exposure to fruits and vegetables from other countries that continue to be requested. I know many of you rely on bananas every morning for breakfast. But the system basically discourages us from eating seasonally appropriate foods, feeding the economies of the imports. Let's come back to this discussion later in the book.

BE IN THE KNOW
Many people believe researching the source of your food is complicated or reserved for fancy people who can afford expensive grocery items. It does not have to be that way.

---

5   The SOFA Team and Cheryl Doss, "The role of women in agriculture," ESA Working Paper No. 11-02 (2011), 1-46.

Of course, the resources available to you depend on where you live, your financial resources, and, really, how much you cook. If you eat out, many chefs are open to educating patrons on what they are eating and where it comes from. When in doubt, ask! And in all fairness, I hope you'll be told the truth.

I realize shifting society-wide priorities might take time in a world where we strive for instant gratification. But what happens when we won't be able to be gratified? The average age of a farmer is nearly sixty years old.[6] What will we do as their farming abilities dwindle?

I am compelled to write this book in order to share the stories of several food heroes, including chefs, farmers, scientists, and food writers. Simply put, the food we eat would not exist without them. They have blazed the trail for those of us interested in this genre to continue their revolution to educate on the relationship humans have with the food we eat. By understanding these relationships, you will learn how to be food detectives and listen to your meals' stories. In doing so, I will empower you to make tasty, responsible, sustainable choices.

For the sake of your own health and that of the land around you, own the source. Go *past* the labels and listen.

This book will help you discover the story behind your favorite meal. You will understand its relevance as you care about

---

6   "Average age of US farmer climbs to 57.5 years," Farm Progress, April 22, 2019.

the quality of its source. Even though I am not a certified nutritionist, you will learn to care for nutrition while learning about the ethics of how it's produced. You will learn about choosing organic. You will learn how to make an impact once you circle back to the moral of the story, your favorite meal. You can then tell your own stories.

As I mentioned earlier, it does not have to be complicated or fancy. We have lost what used to be celebrated: native, local, seasonal, home-processed food. Because our mainstream consumer lifestyle has changed to favor excess, we have strayed from the simplicity of the milk delivery, the daily market stop for fresh unpackaged food, and the luxury of the *occasional* steak. We are out of touch with our food (re) sources. Many books and articles have already been written to encourage people to eat delicious, healthy, and more sustainable food, but my mission is to empower you to understand the *story* of your food. I will bridge the gaps for you with help from the trailblazers, prominent food storytellers, and experts including Dan Barber, Joel Salatin, and Michael Pollan.

Let's work together to create an understanding of sustainability—one that supports us, the animals we eat, and the environment during this time when it seems harder and harder to do so. I will show you it is easier than you think.

If you were interested in this topic before you picked up this book, you might have already started listening to your food. And if you haven't, welcome! I appreciate your curiosity and look forward to taking you on this journey. If you are familiar with the produce referred to as the "Dirty Dozen," if you buy or raise grass-fed beef, if you buy or produce pasture-raised eggs, if you get overwhelmed while you're shopping at the supersized market, if you care about the food products you buy—where they come from, who raised them, how they've been modified to please you—please read on. This book is for you—the curious, concerned, conscientious consumer.

I will explore the intersections of sustainability and the cattle industry, food as community, how to support local/small farmers when it is more expensive and/or you do not have the access (either financial or regional), and food production/ choice during climate change (or a pandemic). You will learn how to support soil as the hero of all beings and what really goes into building a favorite meal. You will hear inspiring stories from Polyface Farm, Apricot Lane Farms, The Savory Institute, Stone Barns Center for Food and Agriculture, and the Soil Carbon Cowboys. We will have conversations pertaining to soil health, covering everything from the beef industry to cheesy garlic bread.

Let us get quiet, band together, and listen.

CHAPTER 1:

HOW WE GOT HERE

_____

The industrial eater is, in fact, one who does not know that eating is an agricultural act, who no longer knows or imagines the connections between eating and the land, and who is therefore necessarily passive and uncritical—in short, a victim.

—WENDELL BERRY; AUTHOR, INSPIRATION
FOR ALL THINGS FARMING AND FOOD

THE STATE OF AFFAIRS

By the year 2050, there will be two billion *more* people to feed.[7]

Due to the present limitations on our natural resources, that is going to be difficult.

I know that's not your responsibility, but it starts with us, as individuals. It starts with surveying our choices and

_____

7   "Growing at a slower pace, world population is expected to reach 9.7 billion in 2050 and could peak at nearly 11 billion around 2100," United Nations, June 17, 2019.

choosing local foods that don't travel around the world. It starts with purchasing foods with less packaging. It starts with meal planning, buying only what is needed, and composting to reduce the amount of food waste in landfills. It starts with knowing where and how our food is produced so we can reduce our carbon footprint. It can start with eating less meat, particularly beef.

THE MAINSTREAM CONSUMER LIFESTYLE

According to the documentary *Why Do We Need to Change Our Food System?*[8], many limitations exist under our current system. Before we move forward with healthier choices, it's important to understand where we are coming from and why these practices are better left behind.

Some data:

- **Worldwide:** One-third of the population suffers from malnutrition.[9] Almost eight hundred million people are hungry.[10] Two billion people do not have sufficient access to vitamins and minerals to assist with appropriate physiological growth.[11]

---

8   "Why do we need to change our food system?" (France: United Nations Environment Programme, 2016), multimedia video, 4 minutes.

9   "Hunger Statistics," World Food Programme, accessed May 19, 2020.

10 Ibid.

11 James O'Hare, "2 Billion People Lack Proper Vitamins & Minerals—But This Group Wants to Change That," Global Citizen, last modified March 29, 2017.

- **Worldwide:** In stark contrast, 1.9 billion people overeat, and six hundred million people are obese.[12]
  - Overeating and obesity lead to food/lifestyle-related diseases like Type 2 Diabetes Mellitus (T2DM).
    - Within the United States, per the Centers for Disease Control and Prevention, 34.2 million people have T2DM, costing hundreds of billions of dollars per year.[13] People with T2DM are at a moderately higher risk of early death than those without it. Most cases can be prevented by eating a healthy diet and exercising. And for those who are prediabetic, if they change their habits to lose weight, they can cut their chance of becoming fully diabetic in half.[14]

- **Our standard American diet** (SAD—because it is, very) typically includes foods that are too rich in fat, sugar, and salt, with a lot of meat consumption. We are putting a significant burden on our bodies and on resources to produce this type of food.
  - Not only does the SAD negatively impact our health, but it also negatively impacts our environment because we source the majority of our food from rice, corn, wheat, cows, chickens, and pigs.
    - Livestock production for food and the food consumed by the livestock produce significant

---

12 "Malnutrition is a world health crisis," World Health Organization, accessed May 19, 2020.

13 "Diabetes in the United States—A Snapshot," Centers for Disease Control and Prevention, accessed May 19, 2020.

14 Ibid.

amounts of greenhouse gas (GHG) emissions.[15] Poultry, pork, and eggs are roughly equivalent in terms of environmental impact. But conventional beef counts for five times as much![16]

- **Our natural resources** are under pressure:
  - Water is very expensive, especially in California, where I live. And very politicized. Our water resources are decreasing from drought and pollution.
  - Thirty-three percent of our soil has degraded, creating food that lacks nutrients and doesn't resemble the food our great-grandparents ate.[17]
  - Deforestation threatens biodiversity to provide more grazing and farm land and increases the drive for gigantic monoculture farms sustained by the four major seed holders (which are chemical companies!).
  - All of which is exaggerated by climate change.
    - Some would call it climate chaos. January 2020 was the hottest January on record.

One-third of all food is wasted (in the US and across the world).[18] This seems so backward when so many are malnourished and hungry. Also, this is even more destructive

15 "Major cuts of greenhouse gas emissions from livestock within reach," Food and Agriculture Organization of the United Nations, September 26, 2013.

16 Rachel Newer, "Raising Beef Uses Ten Times More Resources than Poultry, Dairy, Eggs or Pork," Smithsonian Magazine, July 21, 2014.

17 "Soils are endangered, but the degradation can be rolled back," Food and Agriculture Organization of the United Nations, December 4, 2015.

18 Food Loss and Food Waste," Food and Agriculture Organization of the United Nations, accessed May 19, 2020.

to the environment than the worldwide production of beef. The wasted food sits in the landfills, very slowly emitting methane as it decomposes. It can take a head of lettuce up to twenty-five years to decompose.[19]

The food waste happens at every link of the food chain. It starts at the farm, which doesn't pick or ship all of its supply because the product doesn't fit into the category of "perfect" for the consumer. Therefore, what's "ugly" goes back into the ground as compost. Then, at the market, we are used to seeing abundant choices. Here, also, what's "ugly" gets overlooked. Guess what folks, it tastes the same! Luckily, food delivery services that focus on gleaning these castaways exist. Keep in mind, the food is still traveling across the country, but they are doing a pretty awesome service. Check out Imperfect Foods and Misfits Market.[20, 21]

According to the United Nations Food and Agriculture Organization, if food waste was its own country, it would be third in line of producing the most GHG emissions (behind the US, which is in first, and China in second).[22]

---

19 *Wasted! The Story of Food Waste,* directed by Anna Chai and Nari Kye (2017; New York, NY: Zero Point Zero), documentary.

20 "Grocery Delivery for Organic Food, Fresh Produce & More," Imperfect Foods, accessed May 19, 2020.

21 "Ugly and Imperfect Produce, Delivered to Your Door," Misfits Market, accessed May 19, 2020.

22 "Food wastage footprint—Impacts on natural resources," Summary Report 2013, Food and Agriculture Organization of the United Nations, accessed May 19, 2020.

Each year, more than one billion tons of food are thrown away throughout the world, representing 3.3 billion tons in annual carbon dioxide emissions.[23] This equates to a family of four throwing away $1,800.[24]

Some suggestions to reduce waste:

- Despite me being biased toward fresh local food, do not be afraid to freeze your food or buy frozen, especially if you want blueberries in December or asparagus in October. With the technology of flash freezing, the nutrients are mostly equivalent to those in fresh produce, especially if the produce has traveled far in refrigeration. Also, it prevents you from creating science experiments in your crisper drawer or having a quick reheat of leftovers if you feel too tired to cook. Keep in mind frozen food loses its quality over time, so be sure to eat what you've bought frozen or frozen yourself within two to three months.[25]
- Reduce what you buy. Reuse or repurpose. That roasted chicken can be turned into tacos, which can be turned into taco salad. Recycle or recover by composting or burning for fuel/warmth. Think of the landfill as being the last resort for your food.

The system—including food production, processing, distribution, and consumption—needs to be adjusted to ensure healthier food practices that sustain a reduced environmental

23 Ibid.

24 Dana Gunders, "Wasted: How America Is Losing Up to 40 Percent of Its Food from Farm to Fork to Landfill," NRDC, August 16, 2017.

25 "Are You Storing Food Safely?" US Food & Drug Administration, accessed May 29, 2020.

impact are encouraged. We have the ability to change it! These examples represent the importance of bringing all stakeholders together to produce and eat food differently to decrease GHG emissions, improve overall health, and decrease overconsumption while focusing on increasing biodiversity.

Without the biodiversity of plants and animals, we die.

BIG VS. SMALL

Unfortunately, there is a sense that shopping at farmers markets or subscribing to Community Supported Agriculture (CSA) is associated with hippy, liberal food snobs. I hope this book will loosen your grip on that belief. Because how can you really have a relationship with your food if you don't have an understanding of where it came from? The food I hope ends up on your plate begins on a farm, not in a factory or a laboratory.

The small farm has a very difficult time abiding by the regulations that the larger processing plants do because they are—but really shouldn't be—treated equally by the United States Department of Agriculture. For instance, a rancher in Wisconsin might have to drive miles past one of these smaller slaughterhouses or smaller processing plants in order to get to one that is a USDA-provided plant. The farmer has worked tirelessly to raise these animals humanely and then they get dropped off at these larger facilities that, most likely, do not take as much care with the finishing and processing and, you know, slaughtering of the animals.

So, do your best to research and ask to make sure what you're getting is as much of a humanely processed animal as possible. Not everybody can control that, unfortunately, so until the small production farmer can be allowed to process their own meat on their own farm, we're going to be dealing with those larger facilities that may or may not care. For them, it's not about the treatment of the animal; it's about the job being done.

I am afraid for the smaller farmer.

I mention Joel Salatin more in The Storytellers. His answers regarding challenges pertaining to small family farms have not changed since 2003. There are so many regulations in the United States—not to mention the lobbyists who feed into the larger corporations like Conagra and Bayer. The system seems so incestuous, in terms of the government entities that support these larger companies. We do live in a capitalist society where it is all about "Show Me the Money!"[26] (not the last movie reference). I am afraid the small farmer won't be able to compete and, therefore, the number of farms will continue to decrease.

For instance, previously introduced storyteller Dan Barber and co-author Karen Stabiner wrote an article in *The Counter* discussing the results of Barber's monthlong survey of small

---

26 *Jerry Maguire,* written and directed by Cameron Crowe (1996; Culver City, CA: TriStar Pictures), film.

production farmers throughout the United States.[27] The survey asked the farmers if they foresee still being in operation at the end of 2020. One-third said no due to probable bankruptcy, because they cannot keep up with increasing volume. Others were concerned about not being able to meet the demand of summer and fall harvest because of the inability to keep up with crops, deprivation of labor, and proper cold storage facilities.

As food detectives, we can join in the movement to embrace Barber's idea of a "new food culture that supports diverse small farms and tells the big brands to back off."

As I stated earlier, the average age of a farmer is almost sixty years old, but most of the responders of Barber's survey were between thirty-five and forty-four years old.[28] So, we need to support the younger farmers and hopefully, today, the older farmers have their kids involved in the process. I hope there can be subsidies for the smaller farmers, not just those supported by the lobbyists in there focusing on the larger scale farms that are usually owned by "Monsanto," the name now used interchangeably to refer to any one of the major chemical/big food companies.

---

27 Karen Stabiner and Dan Barber, "Nearly a third of small, independent farmers are facing bankruptcy by the end of 2020, new survey says," *The Counter*, May 18, 2020.

28 "Average age of US farmer climbs to 57.5 years," Farm Progress, accessed May 19, 2020.

THE ALMIGHTY AND POWERFUL SUPERMARKET

Do you get as overwhelmed as I do when surrounded by thousands and thousands of items stacked floor to ceiling? I might be an extremist, but when I walk through those huge stores, all I see is the waste in the landfills: all of the plastic packaging, the jars of expired sauces, the stale cereals, the steamy heads of wilted lettuce. My husband rolls his eyes at me when we walk through a big box store as I remark about feeling claustrophobic. But we do shop there. And we do shop at our local supermarket at least twice per week. We frequent the Sunday farmers market or our local farm stand every weekend. I am not perfect (hello, Trader Joe's frozen Indian food) nor do I one-hundred percent practice what I preach. This book is for me just as much as it is for you. It is a struggle. I am very aware.

I recently met a woman in her sixties who had never been inside a Costco. To me, that's like saying, "I've never seen a sunset." How is that possible? But she stated she had never needed one. She lived close enough to a grocery store and farmers market (open Tuesdays and Saturdays) that supplied her daily needs, and she was able to cook fresh food daily and from scratch for her family. I imagine she is already living this book and is, therefore, ahead of the curve. Round of applause!

Despite giving you the nudge to push past the labels and really listen, I know it is difficult to do so. It takes time and practice. My hope is that reading this book will give you the tools to speed up the process, even if you eat very simply. There are so many options and advertisements following us around the store, all with different marketing ploys that promise to improve any aspect of your life imaginable, many of which are especially effective on you when you're hungry. (Don't ever go to the market hungry!)

The supermarket holds an extreme amount of power. Through marketing or advertising, it controls the majority of the food sales in most developed countries and determines what consumers might not necessarily need but does an excellent job of convincing them they do. For instance, I mentioned Trader Joe's. When I asked where people tend to buy ingredients for their favorite meal, the majority stated Trader Joe's. Cost and value drive the decision on what to shop for and where to shop. Overall, I like the model of Trader Joe's because it has removed most fees (slotting, marketing, middlemen) in order to save on its processes and pass that savings on to the customer.[29]

It buys directly from suppliers and buys in large quantities in order to keep its costs low. Also, it continues to rotate products and use its consumers as its testers—if something does not get bought often, it is discontinued. And, its private label is free of trans fats, artificial colors, artificial flavors, artificial preservatives, and genetically modified ingredients (GMOs). Recently, it released its 2019 Sustainability Progress report on January 1, 2020.[30] It is worth the read.

Though we used to spend our entire day working on our food supply, we now spend eight-ish hours at work to pay someone

29   "Our Story," Trader Joe's, accessed May 18, 2020.

30   "2019 Sustainability Progress," Announcements, Sustainability, Trader Joe's, accessed May 28, 2020.

else to produce our food. That money is used very differently, depending on financial means. We all know better food, valued higher with taste and/or nutrition, is more expensive. Unfortunately, not everyone can afford the better food. And not everyone who can afford the better food will buy it due to myriad factors like education level, time, or accessibility. So that's why I wrote this book! To help you and help those around you pay attention and listen.

Also, Americans have shifted where they spend their money. In 1950, the typical household spent less than 30 percent of their money on food.[31] Americans today spend 10 percent of their salary on food.[32] Mind you, things have significantly changed, hence the need for this book. That means it is even more imperative to listen to the journey so you know you're adding value to yourself by making good choices *and* adding value back to the earth. It might seem complicated, but all it takes is some thought, patience, and wise use of your resources.

I recently had a conversation with my older brother, David. He told me two stories about food. One was of growing up in Washington, D.C., when all my mother and he could get in the wintertime for produce was canned, frozen, or frozen and thawed, which was not the most appetizing. He could not recall any fresh foods offered. And it was even worse for my sister-in-law, Jennie, growing up in Wyoming. Her family canned almost everything to provide food for the wintertime.

---

31   Sterling Price, "Average Household Cost of Food," ValuePenguin by lendingtree, accessed May 19, 2020.

32   Ibid.

Both David and Jennie were excited come spring and summer when food was fresh. Ah, the benefits of regional seasonal eating.

The other story is of when my nephew was little and attending a Montessori school in South Florida. At one of the parent meetings, people discussed what the children should be eating. One of the dads suggested choosing/supplying food *only* from Whole Foods Market because Publix, his local grocery store, could not possibly provide good enough food for the children. David was incensed because a) he had never eaten bad produce from Publix, b) he could not afford to buy everything from Whole Foods Market, and c) Publix had an organic section, so why pay more for the same product labeled as such elsewhere?

My brother's stories are typical of the American experience, both past and present. Luckily, most grocery stores or supermarkets now supply both organic and local. Yes, it is more expensive, but so worth it. And keep in mind those local farmers, even without the organic label, may not be using synthetic pesticides and fertilizers. A little dollop of detective work, either in the store or at home, will enable you to determine where those products are from so you can choose if you want those "fresh" blueberries in January. We'll talk more about this in the Organics chapter.

SPRINGTIME, 2020

Let's bring it back to the current state of affairs. At the time of writing, we've been living through an interesting, very fragile set of circumstances. Our food system has been further challenged by the spread of the COVID-19 virus. Orders of "shelter in place" and "stay at home" initially created an overwhelming hoarding and groupthink mentality. Toilet paper, paper towels, hand sanitizer, and Clorox-based cleaning products are still either limited to one per person or haven't been replenished since early March. People emptied grocery stores of canned goods, boxes of rice, pasta, and sauces. Bread and milk went next, with people freezing any surplus. Then, flour and yeast went, which also continue to be difficult to find. I sent two packages of yeast to a friend in L.A. who said it was worth the price of gold.

I guess stress-bingeing salad isn't really a thing.

The bad: There was, and still is, massive panic. No one is untouched by this. Ground zero of the virus is hypothesized to be an open-air food market in Wuhan, China, with the virus passed from bat to human via another animal host.[33] It then rapidly spread from human to human as people traveled around the world. At the time of publishing, close to four hundred thousand people worldwide have died. The consequences are dire as it trickles down the totem pole to those affected the most, mostly less-than-minimum-wage-paid "essential" workers including employees of grocery stores, farms, packaging plants, and transportation companies. JBS and Tyson, two of the largest meat packaging corporations, shut down plants due to sickened workers. On the other hand, because schools and restaurants are closed, growers cannot sell their products because demand has significantly

---

33 "Frequently Asked Questions," Coronavirus Diseases 2019 (COVID-19), Centers for Disease Control and Prevention, updated June 2, 2020.

decreased. Trucks filled with milk are dumping onto Florida fields. Farms are retilling produce back into the soil. Food banks are presently taxed with a significantly larger demand and a finite amount of supply because of holes in the supply chain.

The good: The USDA and Kroger have recently tended to the disruptions in food distribution due to restaurants/food services and schools being closed because of COVID-19. As recently announced by Sonny Perdue, the US Secretary of Agriculture, the USDA planned to buy over $500 million worth of surplus food to distribute to communities and producers in need.[34] Distribution will begin in July 2020.

Perdue stated, "America's farmers and ranchers have experienced a dislocated supply chain caused by the coronavirus. USDA is in the unique position to purchase these foods and deliver them to the hungry Americans who need it most."[35] And Kroger has purchased, through its Dairy Rescue Program, at least 200,000 gallons of milk to be processed and delivered to food banks throughout the US.[36] "At a time when dairy farmers have surplus (raw) milk, we're doubling down in our mission to reduce hunger and waste," said Erin Sharp, Kroger's group vice president of manufacturing.

---

34 "USDA Farmers to Families Food Box," Agricultural Marketing Service, USDA, accessed May 31, 2020.

35 "USDA Announces Additional Food Purchase Plans," Agricultural Marketing Service, USDA, accessed May 20, 2020.

36 "Kroger Launches Expanded Dairy Rescue Program to Support Children and Families During COVID-19," Kroger, accessed May 19, 2020.

More good: People are cooking more than ever. The grocery stores are open. Farmers markets and farm stands are open (at least in Santa Barbara County), which have been my saving grace. People are growing their own food and experimenting with different coverings, like grow tents, for protection in inclement weather or from sun overexposure. People are getting creative with ingredients (sometimes based upon what is available and others by choice) and posting on food blogs and social media. Home deliveries of produce have increased with an uptick in CSA membership.

Because wineries are not open for tastings, our local farm stand has partnered with a local winery, and I can get a red blend or chardonnay along with my greens, citrus, and eggs. Also, a local cattle rancher stopped participating in all of the farmers markets but has chosen our farm stand to sell, so I can get frozen grass-fed beef in one-pound packages. Our local pork producer has added three different types of pork sausage. It is a one-stop shop, and I can see where the food comes from. It is so exciting. I made leek carbonara the other night, inspired by *Top Chef Kentucky*.[37] It was a winner in our house!

This is a perfect time to stop and listen. I picture that gorgeous scene in *Avatar* when the Na'vi are all plugged in to the earth, swaying back and forth.[38] I want you to feel that

---

37   *Top Chef Kentucky*, Episode 3, "Naughty and Nice," aired December 20, 2018, on Bravo.

38   *Avatar*, written and directed by James Cameron, (2009; Los Angeles, CA: Twentieth Century Fox), film.

grounded as you really survey what you need from the market in order to be the healthiest and 100 percent connected to the land.

Things have slowed down. In the beginning of the crisis, I felt compelled to stock up on things I never buy, which was so strange. I knew I was panicking as I meandered through the supermarket buying bagels, fresh lasagna noodles, prepackaged breakfast burritos, coffee, hummus, whole peanuts, firm tofu, flat bread to make pizza, and a gigantic bag of everything-seasoned pretzels. In the same vein, my husband simultaneously shopped at a different store and bought multiple packs of fresh ravioli, huge containers of nuts, and some Filipino boxed pastry mix. Luckily, all except the nuts and pastry mix has been consumed and we can return to being conscious about our choices, supporting our local farms while eating seasonally, and taking advantage of the abundance.

CIRCLING BACK

Use what you have access to. Take a few deep breaths as you enter the store or market, have a plan, and don't get enticed by the gimmicks or ploys. Remember the advice to prevent waste; it's also a good way to save money. We've heard it before regarding nonfood items, but it pertains here:

- Reduce. Reuse. Recycle. It isn't complicated. Buy only what you need. Think of how many different ways you can use what you're buying. If possible, find a neighborhood garden or botanic garden that will welcome your food scraps. Prevent it from going into the landfill.

- "You are what you eat." You, and you alone, know what makes you and your family feel or behave best. But if you can stay connected to the land, knowing your meal is made from farm-raised ingredients, you are taking a giant step forward toward doing your part and being a conscientious consumer.

Despite a new way of looking at food as we navigate through the dilemma of choosing between continuing to shelter at home or venturing out to support the local economy, my message remains the same in all circumstances:

- It is imperative to those of us sustaining life on this planet to understand our current food system is broken.
- We all have a relationship with our food and benefit from knowing where it comes from in order to do our part to fix the system.
- It falls on us to take more responsibility and empower ourselves to make the best food choices possible—for ourselves and the environment.

I send out heartfelt condolences to any of you who have suffered, lost loved ones, or know of people who have died because of COVID-19.

CHAPTER 2:

THE STORYTELLERS

People are hungry for stories. It's part of our very being.

—STUDS MERKEL; PULITZER PRIZE AUTHOR, BROADCASTER, STORYTELLER

That "Six Degrees of Kevin Bacon" game is a real thing. Here, though, there's a Kevin, but there may or may not be bacon.

In this book, the degrees are more like zero, especially when homing in on sustainable practices and researching the philosophers of simple food while focusing on animal (and human) welfare. Three of these experts are the Storytellers and will help trailblaze your journey through this book: Farmer Joel Salatin, chef Dan Barber, and author Michael Pollan. They represent the practices of pioneers Sir Albert Howard, Wendell Berry, Alice Waters, and the slow clean food movement, the basis of being able to learn your meal's journey. I wouldn't necessarily say these men are friends, (they could be), but I do have to mention a few of the parallels that tickled me as I wrote this book:

- 2002: Pollan visited Salatin at his farm, Polyface Farm, wrote about it in essay form, and incorporated those essays into *The Omnivore's Dilemma*.[39]
- 2003: Salatin and Barber flew to London to attend what Salatin called "a visionary forum" to discuss the past, present, and future of the clean food movement with other experts gathered from around the world.
- 2004: Pollan wrote the foreword for Salatin's *Holy Cows and Hog Heaven: The Food Buyer's Guide to Farm Friendly Food*.[40]
- 2008: Pollan and Barber participated in "Hedonistic, Healthy and Green" at the 92nd Street Y in New York City. Moderated by Joan Dye Gussow, one of the first experts on "eat locally, think globally," it was a discussion on choosing real food grown and raised by real farmers instead of processed foods with origins on factory farms.
- 2008: Salatin and Pollan were featured in the documentary *Food, Inc.*[41]
- 2008: Pollan includes Salatin and Barber in his acknowledgments in his novel *In Defense of Food*.[42]
- 2017: Barber, Pollan, and Salatin were three of seventeen authors who contributed to *Letters to a Young Farmer*,

39 Michael Pollan, *The Omnivore's Dilemma* (New York: Penguin Press, 2006), 8, 123.

40 Joel Salatin, *Holy Cows & Hog Heaven* (Swoope: Polyface, Inc., 2004), xii-xv.

41 *Food, Inc.*, directed by Robert Kenner, written by Robert Kenner, Elise Pearlstein, and Kim Roberts (2008; New York, NY: Magnolia Pictures, Participant, River Road Entertainment), documentary.

42 Michael Pollan, *In Defense of Food: An Eater's Manifesto* (New York: Penguin Press, 2008), 204.

the first book from the Stone Barns Center for Food and Agriculture.[43]

Along with inspiring me, they continue to inspire and refer to each other with their speaking engagements and writing contributions. I want to bridge the gaps for you so you don't have to watch and read everything. Through sharing their stories, you'll understand why they are such inspirations to me and to so many modern food writers, activists, and advocates. They have put in the work. And despite some of the literature being almost twenty years old, it is still relevant because the philosophy doesn't change even as the world around us does.

JOEL SALATIN, FARMER, REPRESENTATIVE OF THE SMALL FAMILY FARM

What I want you to know is that Joel Salatin is a sixty-two-year-old storyteller who performed in high school plays and was on the debate team. These skills have come in handy as he has battled bureaucracy and government encroachment. He is certainly a visionary, but he's had to face confusion, uncertainty, and frustration in order to find resolution (and forgive) without shutting an eye to the rules put in place for small production farmers.

He comes across as somewhat cynical and addresses himself as a Christian libertarian environmentalist capitalist lunatic, rubbing some folks "the wrong way" but delighting others

---

43 Martha Hodgkins, ed., *Letters to a Young Farmer: On Food, Farming, and Our Future* (New York: Princeton Architectural Press, 2017), 59, 72, 112.

with his no-nonsense, almost free-write (many words strung together) way of speaking.

For instance, he recently had two people walk out of his speaking events. One, he assumed, was a non-meat eater who left when he questioned why you'd want to eat a "mono-culture chemicalized GMO soybean-extracted lab percolated earthworm-killing soil-destroying pseudo-food like the Impossible Burger."[44] The second person walked out upon Salatin questioning the US's cultural assumption that a bureaucrat needs to sniff and smell every morsel of food to make sure it's safe for consumption. That person happened to be a government-appointed food inspector. Pause for the "Debbie Downer" theme music. Wouldn't you be slightly cynical too if you've witnessed less and less tolerance to opposing views?

Despite the older nature of his books, specifically *Everything I Want to Do Is Illegal: War Stories from the Local Food Front* and *Holy Cows and Hog Heaven,* they are still relevant.[45, 46] They provide education for the non-farmer food consumer who is conscientious about where food comes from and how it is treated.

I appreciate his integrity as he educates readers on the righteous way to produce food. There is an unrighteous way and a righteous way. Unrighteous means behavior that is

---

44 Joel Salatin, "Stomping Out," *Musings from the Lunatic Farmer* (blog), October 4, 2019.

45 Joel Salatin, *Everything I Want to Do Is Illegal: War Stories from the Local Food Front* (Swoope: Polyface, Inc., 2007), 28-48.

46 Joel Salatin, *Holy Cows & Hog Heaven*, 70, 125.

disrespectful toward our animal stewards, prompting poor health for animals, land, and consumers. Righteous means it ultimately heals with food; it takes care of the bodies of the consumers and considers earthworm health and population, which are important to the health of the soil due to their castings, which provide nutrients and bulk to the soil. This builds layers to the soil, maintains the hydrologic cycle of water, and retains raindrops with decreased topsoil loss with runoff.

In his book *Everything I Want to Do Is Illegal: War Stories from the Local Food Front*, Salatin discussed the trip to London with chef Dan Barber in 2003. After having deep food conversations, the forum tackled the question, "What is the biggest impediment facing your farm specifically and the nonindustrial food system generally?"[47] People stated labor, organic food trafficking, seed regulation, and consolidation. When it came Salatin's turn to speak, he stated, "Everything I want to do is illegal."

Everyone laughed, but he was serious. After the laughter died down, Salatin described how difficult and inefficient the USDA regulations have made on-farm processing of animals, providing on-farm education and seminars, collaborative marketing with other local artisans, employing interns, building a house how he wants to, and opting out of the system. He explained how worried he was when he received a letter from a governmental agency, expecting another roadblock to producing what had once been celebrated: local, indigenous, home-processed food. From that

---

47 Joel Salatin, *Everything I Want to Do Is Illegal*, 2-11.

discussion, upon returning to his farm, he wrote an essay for *Acres USA* of the same title, which was published in the September 2003 issue; it has been his most quoted essay.[48]

Fast forward to 2020. I asked Salatin to similarly explain the biggest challenges facing farming today. He answered, "The biggest challenges facing farming are overburdensome government regulations that preclude entrepreneurs from accessing their neighbors with better food than you can find in the supermarket. Food regulations are all scale discriminatory, which prejudices small operations and concessionizes big operations. We desperately need freedom of choice in the food sector so that voluntary consenting adults may engage in consensual commerce without bureaucrats intervening between lips and throat. This has not changed with the coronavirus."

You have to have deep convictions to be successful in farming when so many others are pulling out of the business. Young people are having difficulty buying in to existing farming infrastructure as experienced farmers are aging. Land purchase is almost impossible due to the expense. Within the next fifteen years, 50 percent of all agriculture equity—land, buildings, machinery—will change hands, older to younger, which means 400 million acres of farmland, an area roughly four times the size of California.[49, 50] "Quite simply: Our future hinges on the investments we make today in the next generation of farmers," he wrote in *Letters to a Young*

---

48 Ibid., 3.

49 Joel Salatin, *Holy Cows & Hog Heaven*, 98.

50 "About," Letters to a Young Farmer, accessed May 30, 2020.

Farmer.[51] That has never happened in any civilization in a time of peace; it has only happened in a time of conquest. Salatin suggests this is a disruptive time and new territory. "No civilization has ever had that level of agrarian wealth transfer." I really hope we will know what to do.

Fortunately, Salatin's Polyface Farm in Swoope, Virginia, exists as the leading example of regenerative farming. I bet you can find one similar in your region to support. Polyface acts as a headquarters for many educational events, and Salatin continues to speak at national and international conferences throughout each year. Farmers and wannabes learn about his holistic farming practices producing meat he describes as "beyond organic," which comes from animals raised using what he describes as environmentally responsible, ecologically beneficial, sustainable agriculture.

Salatin fell out of love for the FDA's Organic certification movement. He predicted early on that the movement would create infighting instead of collaboration and would hurt the smallest farmers. We'll touch upon this in the chapter Choosing Organic, or Not. Polyface has always practiced organically; it refrains from using pesticides or herbicides and fertilizers; it composts. Look up *Salad Bar Beef.*[52] It's incredible.

As a self-proclaimed wannabe, I was thinking about what keeps Salatin going every day. When reading his words or listening to him, you understand the passion behind what

51   Ibid.
52   Joel Salatin, *Salad Bar Beef,* (Swoope: Polyface, Inc., 1995).

keeps it all going. Luckily, he has a constant flow of interns and speaking events to break up the daily workflow and assist with revenue for the farm enterprise. Learning what gets him out of bed every day continued to put things into perspective for me, since my life is so different from his.

> "What gets me up in the morning is the privilege and honor of being able to step out on the back porch and know that I can immerse myself as a participant in Creation's abundance to actually caress our ecological umbilical and tease out the abundances."
>
> — JOEL SALATIN

He told me, "My greatest inspiration comes from seeing the land heal, touching it and watching it come to life."

At the heart of it all, Salatin calls himself a Native American by representing the best of land stewardship and food nutrition. He upholds the integrity of our food culture as being absolutely against government meddling in our system, supporting those who care to be guardians of their own food. He is motivated by customers who have changed their health trajectory by changing their provenance and the thousands of farmers who have found their models lifechanging. He continues improving to help more people do better.

Push aside the politics and find me one person who isn't intrigued with the patriarch of a farm that started out with land where you couldn't find the earthworms. The ground was brick hard. Now you can come out in spring and smell the deep chocolate earth and hear the earthworms moving the soil. Such an awesome transformation.

DAN BARBER, CHEF, REPRESENTATIVE OF INNOVATIVE FARM-TO-TABLE COOKING

What do emmer wheat, a fish, and foie gras all have in common? I'll tell you, but first I'm going to tell you a story. You'll understand a little more about why I want to share with you all I have learned.

It was late fall of 2005 when I ate at Blue Hill in New York City. Blue Hill had been very highly rated since its opening in 2000, with part-owner and executive chef Dan Barber featured numerous times, presenting beautiful plates of farm-to-table food and educating the public at Stone Barns agriculture center in Westchester, New York. I had no idea what to expect, but I was excited. Here was this restaurant that embodied everything I loved about the New York food scene and culture, and it was accessible to me. I knew I would remember it as exceptionally special because no one else was creating what he was. Barber was (and still is) using all parts of his ingredients, showcasing them just as they were, in all their forms. Not only do I remember walking down the stairs into the restaurant, how dimly lit it was inside, how close the tables were placed creating a moderate buzz throughout, and how well our server knew the menu, but also how sophisticated everything appeared and how my excitement turned into embarrassment, like I might be in over my head.

During those years, I was following a vegetarian diet. It surprised me that Barber did not offer a full vegetarian plate on his menu. As I've now learned, he does not promote a full vegetarian diet, stating meat is an important part of the symbiotic relationship with the land producing the food, deserving a role on the plate, even if secondary. I did ask for a vegetarian plate and he obliged. What came out for my entree was a well-seasoned, thick cauliflower "steak" with a root vegetable sauce. It was delicious. And it was cauliflower! I didn't miss the meat.

In between dinner—and maybe dessert—I used the restroom. The pathway to the restroom passes a door that swings open to the kitchen. Just as I walked by, the door swung open. I could see Barber in his chef's whites standing still for a brief second, staring at me. Well, he was probably looking past me, but I felt like he was looking straight at me. Chef Barber is lanky, fast-talking, and unable to be still for prolonged periods of time. You can tell he is constantly thinking. Some people get starstruck by celebrities. Chefs are my celebrities. In slow motion my brain said, "Thank you so much for making me that special entree," but the words got stuck in my throat. Instead, a gurgled "hello" came out along with immediate blushing and a rush into the restroom. When I returned to my seat, there was no door action, and I couldn't redeem myself. I have not received the opportunity to do so to this day.

Despite creating his own catering company in college, Barber did not attend college for culinary education. But he had quite the early cooking career, making his way through kitchens across the country, eventually returning to Manhattan. He first experienced farm-to-table food growing up at his grandparents' farm in the Berkshires of Massachusetts. He took the name of this farm for his restaurants. He is chef and co-owner of *Blue Hill* in *Manhattan* and *Blue Hill at Stone Barns* in *Pocantico Hills, New York*, and sits on the board of the Stone Barns Center of Food and Agriculture.

Blue Hill opened in 2000 in the West Village of Manhattan. Here, he began to develop his signature approach to cooking, looking for locally and sustainably sourced ingredients. This got the attention of David Rockefeller, who hired Barber to take over the responsibility of revitalizing his 3500 acre estate in Westchester, New York, which became Stone Barns Center for Food and Agriculture. Here, with his team, he chooses to put his head down and work toward his high standards for himself. At the end of the day, awards do not make his food taste better. So what does? His quest for a new way of looking at agriculture, "one in which we stop treating the planet as if it were some kind of business in liquidation."[53]

Here is why I want you to know about Barber and why he is so important to the farm-to-table culture: Barber shares his quest for diversity with stories of food and with food. One of my favorites is the one about a fish. Nowadays, many chefs who serve farm-driven cuisine face an ethical dilemma about

---

53 Dan Barber, "How I fell in love with a fish." Filmed February 2010 in Long Beach, CA. TED video.

how to put fish on a plate and still feel good about it. Most of us food detectives know that many fish species have been depleted because of overfishing and climate change and that farmed fish can be really disgusting.

During Barber's quest for sustainable seafood, he traveled to Spain, where he ate a delicious but overcooked piece of white fish and pondered how the fish could taste so good despite being overcooked.[54] Then he met Miguel, a biologist and "expert on relationships" at Veta La Palma, a fish farm in the southwestern corner of Spain. It's at the tip of the Guadalquivir river, which flows into the Atlantic Ocean. It has blossomed into a self-sufficient bird sanctuary that judges its success on the health of the predators. It involves no formal feed. The fish feed on natural wild biomass, algae and phytoplankton. The estuary serves as a water purification system, producing cleaner water than what initially enters the marshes. Barber wants us to follow farmers like Miguel who manage farms that are part of the ecosystem in order to restore and produce extensively. These farmers, who are not just producers, are "the ones that are experts in flavor, too."

While also in Spain, Barber ate the best foie gras he's had in his life.[55] Foie gras means "fat liver" in French and is a delicacy of duck or goose liver that has been forcefully fattened.[56] As of 2008, it was his best culinary experience because of the process and what he observed to be the future of cooking. It

---

54 Ibid.

55 Dan Barber, "A foie gras parable." Filmed July 2008 in Napa, CA. Taste 3 Conference. TED Video.

56 *Encyclopaedia Britannica Online*, Academic ed., s.v. "Foie Gras," accessed May 17, 2020.

was a new idea of using no gavage, also known as force-feeding (usually an animal). These geese and ducks were free to roam about during the warmer months and gorge on food, naturally.

"When my geese feel manipulated, they don't eat as much because they're not happy, but if I give them everything they want, they are happy, so there's no reason for them to leave, and they know it. They feel more comfortable just knowing they are free to go, and they eat more. There's no need to electrify the inside of the fence whereas electrification of the outside protects them by keeping out predators."

—EDUARDO, THE GEESE FARMER

The ducks and geese ate figs, olives, herbs, pepper plants, and the like. Even with the animals eating Lupin seeds, which turned their livers bright yellow—what consumers look for in high-quality foie gras—it "technically" couldn't be considered foie gras because, historically, it is made with gavage (accompanied by a level of cruelty). So, Eduardo was cheating. But the final product was "sweet and unctuous. It had all the qualities of foie gras, but its fat had a lot of integrity and a lot of honesty." Barber realized serving foie gras in his restaurants wasn't possible anymore because what he had access to was nothing near this. And, Eduardo didn't sell to chefs. With Barber's story, Eduardo demonstrated "the most ecological choice for food is also the most ethical choice for food and, almost always, the most delicious choice."

Barber has recently tried his luck at raising geese at Stone Barns for foie gras as close to Eduardo's as possible. But, after failing at the venture, he realized he could raise geese, and use their livers, but not call it "foie gras." "It was me who had failed the geese, not the other way around. . . . It transcends craft. It becomes more than the sum of its parts."[57]

The third part of Barber's quest took him home to New York state to an organic grain farm that produced emmer wheat, which he used for his whole-wheat brioche as a tasting menu course on its own. During a tour of the farm, Barber realized he was going about his buying of the wheat all wrong due to the rotational yields of all different grains, which assisted with making the wheat—a mono crop—delicious. "Standing in Klaas's fields, I saw how single-minded I had been. Yes, I was creating a market for local emmer wheat, but . . . I was cherry-picking what I most wanted for my menu without supporting the whole farm."[58]

How could he live up to his striving for flavor if he wasn't supporting biodiversity at the ground level? Barber learned

57 Dan Barber, *The Third Plate: Field Notes on the Future of Food* (New York: Penguin Books, 2015), 197-198.

58 Dan Barber, "The Chef's Role in the Creation of a Sustainable, Healthy Diet," Filmed November 2014 in Pocantico Hills, NY, 2014 Food for Tomorrow Conference, YouTube video, 10:01-11:27.

there was no set recipe for guaranteed great tasting wheat because, naturally, the process changes daily in order to create the best soil for optimal crop health. Optimal crop health includes the use of rotational grains to maximize the ability of nutrients fixing the soil. So out of the grain rotations he created a riceless risotto, which incorporated about six rotational grains, legumes, and seeds that were used to prep Klaas' soil for the wheat.

An ode to the process.

What also came out of this relationship with the organic grain farmers and other breeders was Barber's propensity toward flavor. "I'm really trying to make my food taste better than I am a talented chef. I mean that's what I drive toward. It always was my original intent to search for the foods with these jaw-dropping flavors because they make me look like a better chef." First, a special strain of wheat known as Barber wheat was developed with "renegade breeder" Steve Jones. And then, in 2010, Barber challenged his vegetable breeder Michael Mazourek to breed a butternut squash for flavor, not yield.[59] No one had asked Mazourek to breed for flavor before. Challenge accepted. The honeynut squash was born—smaller, creamier, sweeter, and denser than the butternut due to less water content. I have yet to try it.

More experts joined their team to create Row 7 Seed Company. "We need to protect seed for what it is: dynamic, living, delicious. If we do it right we'll win," which is hard to believe due to 75 percent of the world's crops disappearing in the last

---

59   "Our Story," Row 7 Seed Company, Accessed May 18, 2020.

one hundred years and chemical companies acting as seed owners, controlling their dissemination very tightly.[60] "The idea behind Row 7 is to upend that calculus by giving chefs a voice from the beginning of the conversation, empowering breeders and farmers to grow diverse, nutritious, and delicious crops."

I know that Blue Hill's menu is different now, ten years later, but the philosophy that I so admire(d) still stands: creating ethical farm-to-table food that is delicious, beautiful, and clean while supporting the smaller production farmers who strive to cultivate healthy crops, animals, and soil, promoting diversity. There are restaurants near you that employ this same philosophy. Go find them!

MICHAEL POLLAN, AUTHOR, ULTIMATE FOOD DETECTIVE

Despite Michael Pollan recently meandering into the world of psychedelics, he continues to be a resource for those of us interested in listening to our food and understanding the origins of the food and why those origins are so important. You could say he was the original food sleuth.

So much of what Pollan has produced over the last thirty years has been inspired by the soil health pioneers: Howard, Berry, Joan Dye Gussow, and Alice Waters.[61] He had his a-ha moment once he understood the importance of soil after his own gardening adventures. As the son of two writers,

---

60 Ibid.

61 Michael Pollan, *In Defense of Food*, 204.

he could have chosen a much different path but naturally received both a BA and MA in English. What he thought would be a profession as an English professor morphed into one where he became a writer, focusing first on how humans exist in and with nature. Luckily for you, that led to researching what, why, and how we eat.

It is difficult not to just list all of the links to his writing contributions and tell you to read them all now and/or state verbatim the most important passages of his books or essays. It is difficult not to feel like an imposter by accessing his mind, through words and video, and resharing the themes that are very meaningful to me and to everyone else who cares for the environment, our bodies, and animal welfare. But I do have to remember all of you may not have read his books or essays.

Therefore, I am grateful he has deeply delved into this realm of responsible stewardship toward the land and humans by offering multiple sources on how to eat the healthiest: "Eat food. Not too much. Mostly plants."[62] Also, if you need to shop in the supermarket, stick to the outer edges; good healthy food starts with good healthy soil; if we have been fattening animals with carbohydrates then, perhaps, we should not be eating them ourselves (let me access my '80s child self: DUHHH); you won't find high fructose corn syrup at the farmers market; sustainability matters; eating seasonal organic local food is the most beneficial thing for everyone and everything.

---

62 Ibid., 1.

Being in the academic world, he has the ability to have research assistants and fact checkers, which assures his readers that a) we are lucky because they have done the hard work and b) what he has written is fair and without bias. From his first book, *Second Nature: A Gardener's Education*,[63] to his most recent food-related book, *Cooked*, he has dedicated countless hours to telling the stories about the journeys of our plates of food and to what we need to pay attention.[64] It has allowed him to take his own journeys and be a part of some exceptional projects, including the Oscar-nominated documentary *Food, Inc.*; documentary adaptations of *In Defense of Food* and *The Botany of Desire*, both on PBS; and a four-part (air, water, fire, earth) series based on *Cooked* on Netflix.[65, 66, 67, 68]

What I have found most beneficial is what Pollan shares in his *Eater's Manifesto: In Defense of Food*.[69] As I've stated, despite these storytellers providing information over ten years ago, nothing has changed. In fact, there are even more

63   Michael Pollan, *Second Nature: A Gardener's Education* (New York: Grove Press, 1991).

64   Michael Pollan, *Cooked: A Natural History of Transformation* (New York: Penguin Press, 2013).

65   *Food, Inc.*, directed by Robert Kenner, written by Robert Kenner, Elise Pearlstein, and Kim Roberts (2008; New York, NY: Magnolia Pictures, Participant, River Road Entertainment), documentary.

66   *In Defense of Food*, directed by Michael Schwarz, written by Edward Gray (2015; Menlo Park, CA: Kikim Media), documentary.

67   *Botany of Desire*, directed by Michael Schwarz, Edward Gray (2009; Menlo Park, CA: Kikim Media), documentary.

68   *Cooked*, directed by Peter Bull, Alex Gibney, Ryan Miller, and Caroline Suh (2016; New York, NY: Jigsaw Productions, Netflix), documentary.

69   Michael Pollan, *In Defense of Food*, 161.

products available in the grocery stores now than there were in 2008, so it's even more valid today. He advises the eater on what to pay attention to if we want to survive on our best meal and live our best life as follows. Here we go with the labels: Be smart.

- Don't eat anything your great-grandmother wouldn't recognize as real food.
  - Go-Gurt, anyone? Or a cheese product? Even Epic Bars—which I think are wonderful because they are trying to be as sustainable as possible by using all parts of the animal—are a mixture put into bar form in a wrapper. All are highly processed.

- Don't eat anything incapable of rotting. Sorry (not sorry), Twinkie.
  - But I have learned, honey doesn't rot. Eat honey! Honey is good.

- Avoid food products containing ingredients that are a) unfamiliar, b) unpronounceable, c) more than five in number or d) include high fructose corn syrup.
  - We all love bread. Pollan uses a Sara Lee brand bread example in the book. I'll use a different one: Brown-berry (the brand) Oatnut Bread.

FIRST OF ALL, WHAT'S AN OATNUT?
Ingredients: **Whole Wheat Flour, Water, Enriched Wheat Flour** [Flour, Malted Barley Flour, Reduced Iron, Niacin, Thiamin Mononitrate (Vitamin B1), Riboflavin (Vitamin B2), Folic Acid], **Oats, Sugar, Wheat Gluten, Yeast, Soybean**

Oil, Hazelnuts, Cultured Wheat Flour, Salt, Sunflower Seeds, Soy Lecithin, Grain Vinegar, Citric Acid, Nuts (Walnuts, Almonds). It comes with the disclaimer: "Contains wheat, soy, hazelnuts (filberts), walnuts, almonds, made in a bakery that may also use milk." It touts "No Added Nonsense," "Whole Grains," No Artificial Preservatives, No Artificial Colors or Flavors, 28g Whole Grains per two slices (I guess they state two because who just eats one slice of bread?)

I would disagree with the "no added nonsense."

- Enriched wheat flour happens to lack important dietary fiber people usually associate with bread to help with improved intestinal motility, but it does have those added vitamins . . . (that aren't needed in your bread if you're eating a well-rounded diet with fruits and vegetables)
- Cultured wheat flour is a natural preservative to enhance flavor and extend shelf life.
- Wheat gluten is added to make the bread more elastic. Whole wheat flour has lower gluten density than white flour.
- Soybean oil is the most used and produced oil worldwide, therefore making it readily available and inexpensive.[70] It adds the fat content, emulsifies, and adds flavor.
- Soy lecithin is a food additive; when added to bread it acts as an emulsifier to improve flavor and prevent staling.

70 University of California—Riverside. "America's most widely consumed oil causes genetic changes in the brain: Soybean oil linked to metabolic and neurological changes in mice." ScienceDaily, January 17, 2020.

- Grain vinegar, also known as distilled white vinegar, is needed to react with the yeast and adds flavor.
- Citric acid is used as a bread conditioner, which gives it more elasticity and extends shelf life.

- Who likes their coffee "light?" Me!
- So, let's also look at nondairy creamer in liquid form:

Ingredients: **Water, Corn Syrup, Soybean & Cottonseed Oil, High Fructose Corn Syrup, Sodium Caseinate, Dipotassium Phosphate, Mono & Diglycerides, Sodium Stearoyl Lactylate**

- Sodium Caseinate, the most common form of the milk derivative casein, is used for fat and water binding and stabilization.
- Dipotassium phosphate prevents clumping.
- Glycerides are used as emulsifiers.
- Sodium stearoyl lactylate is an additive and emulsifier for improved mixing and volume.
  - Others add "artificial flavor," often manufactured from corn.

- Avoid food products that make health claims.
  - Remember, our national "associations" are paid to make health claims for certain foods. Don't believe everything you are told. We go over this in Being the Detectives.
  - And, if there is a claim on the package, it's in a *package* and has been at least a little processed—therefore, not a whole food.

- Shop the periphery of the supermarket and stay out of the middle.
  - This was a genius suggestion I have been abiding by, mostly, for many years. And it has helped me to learn new ingredients and eat fewer processed foods.
  - Most supermarkets are laid out the same: fresh foods line the walls while the processed, very shelf-stable foods, line the center aisles.

- And better yet, support your farmers and #getoutofthegrocerystore.[71] (Yes, Niti Bali!)
  - At your local farm stand or farmers market you'll find fresh, healthy, seasonal ingredients. "No old food from far away." You can talk to the farmers or their employees about their practices to learn conventional versus organic. Even if they don't use the label "Organic," many times they are but haven't gone through the bureaucratic steps to acquire the designation. You will be advocating for your health if you ask if they use pesticides. Please do so!
    - "Shake the hand that feeds you!" Now in the time of COVID-19, bump elbows or bow.
  - Much of the organic produce offered in the supermarket is from very far away. You are taking money away from your local/regional farmers.

---

71 Niti Bali, *Farm to Fork Riot* (White River Junction: Chelsea Green, 2019).

"Only when we participate in a short food chain are we reminded every week that we are indeed part of a food chain and dependent for our health on its peoples and soils and integrity—on its health."[72]

—MICHAEL POLLAN

It took me a long while in this process to get through this part of the chapter. It is impossible not to share what Pollan has already witnessed and written about. I found his common themes invaluable, which will continue to be spread throughout this book, along with that of Salatin, Barber, and the other pioneers mentioned earlier. I have shared this information in order to help you take that next step: Push past the labels and really listen to the food regarding where it has been, what it has gone through, how much processing has taken place, and if it is a healthy choice. You are in control. And we are always learning, together, how to be better food sleuths.

TAKEAWAYS:
- The Storytellers are the leading representatives of my inspiration for us to be more like the Native Americans or the indigenous peoples of your home country.
- We are benefitting from the practices learned from their examples of inspirational pioneering trailblazers.

---

72 Michael Pollan, *In Defense of Food*, 161.

- They say we have the ability to celebrate indigenous, locally grown food and to lead by example. And they're right!
- Whether it be with a farm box delivered to your house, the occasional trip to the farm stand, looking for the "Local" label in your grocery store, or celebrating the delicious dinner out at your favorite farm-to-table restaurant, you can benefit from eating righteously and being the least burdensome to the planet.

CHAPTER 3:

THE FAVORITE MEAL — THE CONVERSATION STARTER

Food is everything we are. It's an extension of nationalist feeling, ethnic feeling, your personal history, your province, your region, your tribe, your grandma.

—TONY BOURDAIN; CHEF, AUTHOR, TRAVELER, PHO CONNOISSEUR

Oftentimes at dinner parties, my husband will start a conversation with, "Okay, what's your last meal?"

What is your *last* meal, versus what is your *favorite* meal, evokes different emotions. Although, for some, the answer is the same.

I prefer using "favorite" because it is less heavy and people usually have multiple answers. During my research, this was the first question I asked as a) an ice breaker and b) the explanation that this is the basis of our work as food detectives. It is the basis for this book: taking my favorite plate of food and looking at each component so I can make each one taste its best. Many times, I was asked the question back. My favorite meal is a six-ounce, grass-fed filet mignon cooked in butter with salt and pepper, finished in the oven, served with garlic rosemary mashed potatoes with cream, salted butter, and pepper, and some steamed broccoli with lemon, butter, salt, and pepper.

I love this plate of food. It isn't the most healthful, but it is the one time where I engineer the three components to end at the same time with that final magical bite. Well, maybe I do that at Thanksgiving as well . . . but this, my favorite meal, is perfect. I relish in the initial crunch of the charred sear of the meat, which then melts in my mouth with juicy softness, coupled with the salty creaminess of the potatoes and the brightness of the broccoli, cooked al dente. It completes me (not-so-shameful movie reference).[73]

I can't tell you why it is, other than the fact that the components are magically delicious. I can only imagine that the first time I ate it made a significant impression: at a restaurant, probably a trendy, loud, vibrant New York City steakhouse in my late twenties with my ex and his family. I do not know where the beef was sourced, how it was raised, if the broccoli or the cream used for the mashed potatoes were organic. I do know that, per the price, they *should* have been organic and

---

73 *Jerry Maguire,* written and directed by Cameron Crowe (1996; Culver City, CA: TriStar Pictures), film.

ethically sourced, but it was downtown Manhattan where the food caters more so to the scene than to conscientious eaters.

There are the four components to the favorite meal: what, when, why, and how? The stories included in this chapter answer these questions and equate to a very small sample size but one I thought would represent a good part of the population. The people interviewed range from singles to married couples with multiple children to established authors in the food community, all inspirations to me. Sometimes the food is the central part of the table; other times it's about the people surrounding the food on the table. No matter what, we need nutrients to survive. I included this story-based chapter to tie us all together because we are all connected, often with and by food.

Where do *you* fit? Read on and find out.

WHAT

What, for the most part, is answered somewhat haphazardly for 75 percent of people asked, with lots of verbal processing while filing through the rolodex of all of the meals eaten throughout their lifetime to what evokes the most joy. Twenty-five percent of people answer immediately without backing down despite discussion afterwards. Seasonal, versus community or family driven, versus just plain delicious. At first, the answer is something the person finds delicious, like my meal, but most often, it ends up involving some special component from tradition or family. For instance, my friend Bryan described to me the most perfect, mouthwatering bacon cheeseburger, telling me where to find it in Scottsdale,

Arizona, and how cooking it himself is almost impossible because of the difficulty of getting every component perfect, down to the ratio of bun to ingredients.

But what he really wanted to tell me about was explaining his favorite night of the year: Poppa Pizza Night—celebrating his father, Mike, (who passed away in 2016) with pizza on his birthday. Whenever Mike would come to town, Bryan would turn over the kitchen to him to make pizza with the kids. They blast Jimmy Buffett and break out Bryan's father's recipe from when he had his pizza restaurant in Chicago. Each of Bryan's three children chooses their own toppings— sourced from their garden and/or Whole Foods Market—and helps ladle the sauce, puts on their toppings, and loads up the cheese. Bryan shuffles the pizzas in and out of the oven using a baking sheet. The best pizza, originally called Boston Pie, is now called Summer Pie and has no sauce, olive oil, a light layer of cheese par-baked to be brown and crispy. Then, it's taken out and fresh vegetables (perfect heirloom tomatoes, fresh basil, raw white onion) are added. It is a blast. He loves that they have made it a family tradition.

And speaking of family, my friend Kevin began his favorite meal by stating it's a four-part meal from all over the world, pieced together. (There are no rules here, people.) What was most interesting to me is he spent the most time explaining his mother's cheesy garlic bread after stating his meal would be what is maybe the best thing he's ever tasted in his life: pairing the boeuf bourguignon from Le Diplomate on 14th Street in Washington, DC, with cast iron scalloped potatoes from a restaurant in a tiny village in the south of France, his mother's garlic bread, and his ex's flourless chocolate lava cake with a nice fresh green salad. Maybe or not in that order.

Despite him detailing everything from the sound of the cars in the French village and the crunch of the potatoes to the wine he'd drink with the beef stew in DC and the fact that he misses the lava cake (but not much else), he definitely got my taste buds aflutter when describing his mother's garlic bread. I have never had the pleasure of eating it, and there would be no way Kevin would choose to eat it out of his house due to the ingredients used (sourdough bread, a pre-prepared mixture of Kerrygold butter mixed in with lots of garlic, cheddar cheese added to Kraft Parmesan cheese, plus more cheese bubbling on the top) not being permitted in his mostly Paleo diet. But he states every other component of the meal can change but the bread—it's always there. It's this sign that, even when he's out in the world off doing his own thing, no matter how hard that gets or whether he's had a long travel day to get back, he says,

"Oh, here's this thing that I remember from when I was five and I've had, you know, constantly since then, that I'm now experiencing and it's like, hell, I'm back. I'm around the family and I'm home. I'm around the people that I love and so it is imbued with the weight of love, that those are my people."

—KEVIN

So often, it's the love felt around the dinner table that inspires a favorite meal. But what about making food as love in order to nourish your family? That's what my friend Erika's husband, Brendan, accomplishes. His drive when cooking for his family is to make unprocessed, one-hundred-percent made-from-scratch food. Amazing!

His go-to is chicken soup. I mean, who doesn't like chicken soup? It is versatile and comforting, and there are myriad different versions across many cultures. There is pho, chicken and rice, chicken veggie, etc.—a million different ways. It makes the house smell incredible and homelike. It's a great way to stretch one chicken into a lot of meals—not costly. Humble. When someone really knows how to make it, it's incredible, but even if you're okay at cooking, it is still pretty good.

He sources the chicken from Sage Hill Farms, which is local to Santa Barbara and organic. So, it's more expensive but worth it. For most everything else, he shops at Trader Joe's. But what is remarkable is Brendan and his family of six grow some of their own food, mill flour, and bake their own bread. They have chickens, fruit trees, a garden, and compost. He states his biggest challenge is that the ingredients he wants are much harder to find in Santa Barbara as compared to the Bay Area (where he and Erika used to live). He's learned that the best local ingredients from Santa Barbara go elsewhere. Our local lobsters go straight to China, for example, which I didn't know prior to interviewing him.

Even without blood-related family, food can be special when shared with friends who act like family. This happens when you move to a new city and find yourself alone during the holidays because you cannot afford to go home and/or you're the newest hire and do not have the clout to ask for time off. My friend, Laura (also known as Bucky), experienced this during her first New York City Thanksgiving in 2005. She did not have an established New York family but was invited to one of her dance mentor/instructor's homes. She was working three jobs and taking dance classes to find community.

Bucky is one who associates the gathering that took place—rather than the food on her plate—as a favorite meal. Her friend Ezra, the host, had a huge long table with the cutting board at the top where he cut and mixed foods—even raw meat and chopped garlic. He prepped everything on the table, washed it clean, and set plates down to eat the meal at the same space. It was interesting to her, as an introvert, watching all of this happen while gleaning Ezra's attitude about food, which was about using salt and pepper ("Don't fuck it up!") and making it while *with people*, more than focusing on the fact that he was making holiday food *for people*. Nobody brought things like appetizers or whatnot because he did not organize that kind of thing. His opinion was you just don't (bring appetizers) so people are starving by the time the food eventually comes and they all love it.

And sure enough, Bucky will never take for granted remembering the meal as if choreographed: everyone being in the kitchen the entire time, talking and moving about. And then once the meal was over and Bucky was walking to the subway, the first snow of the year began: just a trickle of snowflakes. That was what sealed the magic of one of her favorite meals.

WHEN

As you listen to your meal's story, much of it has to do with its season. If I were to follow that lead, I should eat my favorite meal during broccoli season, which happens to be January–June in Central/Southern California, despite being able to find it year-round. This brings me to my brother, Paul. His favorite meal rotates because he likes food so much and he tries to eat seasonally. It depends on where he is and the season. Growing up, he went through a phase eating nothing green. And now he's mostly vegan, which always makes me chuckle.

He has eaten seasonally since he lived in Florida because of the Community Supported Agriculture (CSA) farm stand in Jupiter, where he worked. He would drive around South Florida and visit the different farms, going physically to the farmers and seeing what they would grow. In talking to the farmers, he would ask why they didn't grow such and such at that point of the year. For instance, potatoes and rutabaga, root vegetables, squashes in the winter, because they handle the cold much better versus greens that do not grow well in the winter, but were, in fact, terrible in the summer. In the summer, they would get their greens from the Shenandoah Valley because it was too hot to grow anything, like lettuce, in Florida.

But now, Paul lives in Reno, and I interviewed him in October, so he had recently fixed a fruit salad type of thing with tangerines, blood oranges, navel oranges—which he peeled and paired at home with cinnamon—raisins, and plain yogurt. "And that's where I'm at right now. It's about the ultimate for me, and maybe some apples—apples are in season, too. So, I didn't put the apple in yesterday, but I was thinking about getting some apples." He says yes to organic fruits and Wallaby organic Greek yogurt—the whole milk version because, obviously, the whole milk stuff tastes better.

Other meals revolve around the seasons or more so what feels good to eat when you want to be cozy during wintertime or feel fresher and cooler in the summer. For instance, my friend Heather loves to make chicken tortilla soup (another version of Brendan's meal) when it's cold outside and big, gorgeous salads when it's hot.

"Meals can spark the appreciation for the change of the seasons—it's not about eating the meals, it's what makes the meals."

—HEATHER

So, even though she can make these meals year-round, she enjoys making them much more when they are seasonally appropriate, i.e. making a stew or soup in wintertime and eating it with a fire going.

Heather makes her chicken tortilla soup with basic organic chicken stock—not from scratch. "If I was the perfect housewife, I'd make it from scratch. But I buy the free-range organic chicken stock and then add onion, garlic, of course, which is included in everything I cook, and then canned diced green chilies." The chicken is free range organic rotisserie, which she always has on hand, shredded and in the freezer to add into recipes. She sources most of the vegetables from the farmers market for what's in season, and she buys whatever isn't in season from Whole Foods. In an ideal world, she would source her meats from the farmers market to support our local meat community. Perhaps one day she will. Regardless, she'll always opt for organic produce. If it isn't available organically or somewhat locally, she won't use it.

One of the experts featured in this book, Michael Pollan, is similar to Heather. I am grateful for the information he has offered his community of readers and students about nutrition, health, food responsibility, and how not to go too crazy with all of our options. His favorite meal is one that is prepared with some consciousness, mindfulness, and thought. Specifically, and especially in wintertime, it is roast chicken with root vegetables cooked together in one pan with the vegetables underneath the chicken. He takes the backbone out of the chicken and splits it (this method is called spatchcocking) so it is flat in the pan and cooks evenly and more quickly than your typical roasted chicken. The juices flow into the vegetables, infusing them with flavor, helping to cook them quickly. You can make it whenever, specifically midweek when there's "food fatigue" because it takes only forty minutes. It's a great comfort meal.

And he also loves grilling fish outside. Pollan lives in California and can grill all year. He marinates a piece of fish very simply in lemon juice, olive oil, herbs, and garlic for a couple hours, then puts it on the grill for a few minutes. There's nothing better, and it's really simple. Good, healthy, and responsibly sourced (I am *assuming* this because he didn't state its source, but historically eats organically and ethically) food can be comforting and does not have to be complicated.

WHY

Do you know how many items, on average, are in a supermarket? Thirty-five thousand.[74] That equates to infinite combinations of favorite meals. So, what leads us to a place of non-overwhelm as we figure out what we enjoy? There are many answers to this question including taste, affordability,

---

74 "Supermarket Facts," The Food Industry Association, FMI, accessed June 1, 2020.

access, community, and health. As I've told you, taste is what drives my meal. Don't tell anyone, but when I eat my favorite meal, everything else around becomes a blur, as if the plate is highlighted by a spotlight and I am there to relish it, one small bite at a time. Life stops around me. It's very strange. And then my husband asks me a question or says, "Right?" to something he had been previously talking about, and I have to embarrassingly ask him to repeat what he had said. Oops.

Taste and consistency of quality and flavor drives the favorite meals of my friend Brooke. She, like most people, struggled with stating just one plate of food as her favorite. She reminisced about our time living in Queens, New York, when frequenting Taverna Kyclades in Astoria. She would choose as her favorite meal "really yummy fresh Mediterranean food" including the Greek salad with the perfect amount of salt and delicious feta cheese or the grilled octopus with lemon and olive oil. It has to be the right ingredients. Not super processed, so you can taste the flavors of the food coming through. She wants to balance the needs of the day and meal with planetary needs, wanting to make more choices for the planet and less individualized choices because she thinks we'll end up in a better place.

But really, it's about survival. Being healthy and sustaining her health never feels bad. She wants to be conscious of her sourcing in many ways, but there is one exception to her rule: a braised beef taco she gets a few times per week. She does not know from where the small taco stand sources its ingredients, nor does she care. The taco energizes her. It is convenient, quick, and affordable. And tasty.

On the other hand, this gets into a different conversation regarding the survival piece Brooke mentioned. Brooke and her wife are raising three children, a nine-year-old and three-year-old twins. They all eat different foods due to choice and health reasons. Luckily, their oldest is their best model for moderation because she has no addiction to food or sugar. They allow her to eat and read simultaneously, which is the unhealthiest thing she does with food because she doesn't use food to soothe. The twins do not eat much (at the point of our interview), so they can subsist on a few tablespoons of food at a time; therefore, there is no formal dinner for them. (Popsicles are fruit.) And meat is used to sustain energy and balance.

Brooke can control what goes into the mouths of her family, but she is more concerned about the antibiotics fed to cattle than she is about the environmental impact of raising cattle. She acknowledges the meat issue is tricky.

"We are omnivorous creatures and if we are raised without meat we are missing out on core nutrients. I want to give my children the choice to eat or to not eat meat. I like to prepare, offer and step the hell back. It's all about modeling—if you can be a role model, that is what we can be for our kids and those around us. In order to be balanced."

—BROOKE

What better way to be a role model for children than to show them healthy ways to eat as a family and to build community? That's where pizza night comes in. Many of the people I interviewed stated pizza night as their favorite meal. All of the pizza processes discussed support local farms, use organic produce from their own gardens and/or Whole Foods Market, and are made of ingredients from other ethical sources. *Clean Food* cookbook author and educator Terry Walters states, "This is the one meal that brings everyone together."[75] That alone makes it super-nourishing.

Bryan, mentioned earlier, loves to make meals at home, especially when his wife and three children are involved—hence

---

75 Terry Walters, *Clean Food: A Seasonal Guide to Eating Close to the Source* (New York: Sterling Epicure, revised & expanded 2012).

Poppa Pizza Night being so special. And Heather, also mentioned earlier, loves that it allows her to be creative with her toddler and that it marks the beginning of the weekend, when her husband is done with work for the week. "Let's kick back and relax and start our weekend off with a celebratory nature to it." They all ensure the dough is right—either homemade or store-bought—because "pizza is all about the dough."

Speaking of dough, Walters makes a sourdough crust that she ferments for seventy-two hours. They love topping it with just about anything. She most recently made it when her children, about to go back to school, requested it over the holidays. "We had family, friends, and two amazing pizzas that were topped with pesto, spinach, roasted squash, caramelized onions, and maitake mushrooms. Some helped with the prep while others sat around the kitchen island. The lights were dim, with sparkly lights on the beams at each end of the island. It was magical. There was tons of laughter, shouting, music, and even a bit of dancing. The pizza was the centerpiece that made it a party. Like every other time, when there is pizza, there is great joy, togetherness, and love."

Togetherness and love. There is no better answer to "why." Just like what Kevin said earlier about his mom's garlic bread, "It imbues love." Another of my food mentors, Niti Bali, said her favorite meal is one enjoyed together without electronics or gadgets. She states they enjoy one meal like that daily, but the most "lavish" meals are on the weekends. They are able to "enjoy conversations with each other while enjoying a variety of regenerative grilled meats and seafood. The meal is simple but elegant, delicious, nourishing, medicinal, but very simple to prepare and enjoy." Together.

In a time when our United States food system is moving away from celebrating food cooked together in a kitchen using local, whole, organically grown ingredients, I deeply appreciate hearing these stories. Not all mealtimes are equal, but these favorite meals are made not just for the combinations of food flavor but the *gatherings* they require to create the magic in order to make it all taste its best.

HOW

The last component to the favorite meal is how. Easy, right? Buy the food and cook it and eat it. With today's standards in our developed country, it's simple. But there are still folks who have to walk to gather water to cook and/or meander outside to their garden or go into their cellar to choose what's available and cook it. Or the next step removed is to go to the farmers market, choose what's in season, talk to the farmers about their practices, take the ingredients home, and cook. Neither of these scenarios involve tipping unless it's your hat to your neighbor or asking for advice on how to cook a particular ingredient. This takes me to the next removed step in the process: eating out. Many restaurants, thankfully, are opting in to educating their patrons on the sources of their ingredients, how the animals were raised, the difference between conventional versus organic. But most don't.

Just like with the why, we all have choices. We can shop in the supermarket, inundated with the thirty-five thousand products staring at you, saying, "Buy me! Buy me!" We can take them home and assemble either from whole food ingredients or containers heated on the stove, in the oven or microwave, having hopefully saved as much of the nutritional content as possible. So, dare I move on to the most removed step? We can choose to perform a series of clicks in order to have our dinner show up in plastic containers or a big box with everything already portioned out, down to the spices required per each meal. We are getting closer and closer to resembling the humans in the Pixar movie *Wall-E*[76] and Wendell Berry's description of the industrial food consumer: "strapped to a table with a tube running from the food factory directly into his or her stomach."[77]

It's frightening. Hence my need to write this book.

I mentioned Michael Pollan earlier. He approaches the farmers market as a grab bag for yumminess. It is delicious to make a meal from items from the farmers market when you don't know what you what you're going to get and you just walk in to see what grabs your eye. And then you go through that process of wondering, "What can I do with these six things?" If you don't recognize a product, ask the vendor what it is and how to cook it. From conception to cooking to consumption is one continuous set of surprises that is always delicious. (It probably helps that Pollan knows his way around seasoning and the kitchen—always a good resource.) That's often his Thursday night dinner because that is when the farmers market sets up in his neighborhood. Pollan explained, "We start out the day: We have no idea what we're going to have and we see what looks good.

---

76 *WALL-E,* directed by Andrew Stanton, written by Andrew Stanton, Pete Docter, and Jim Reardon (2008; Burbank, CA: Walt Disney Pictures, Pixar, FortyFour Studios), film.

77 Wendell Berry, *Bringing It to the Table: On Farming and Food* (Berkeley: Counterpoint, 2009), 228.

Recently the asparagus came into the market and you know it's so amazing when it's fresh and just shows up."[78]

"Eating in season is part of my ideal meal. I love the fact that tomatoes go away for eight months or so and then come back and how amazing they are and how you forget what an incredible thing a tomato is. The same with asparagus . . . All these things that just have their moment."

—POLLAN

You don't have to be Michael Pollan to be successful with this venture.

Brooke and Heather—and the majority of those interviewed—shop for organic local produce, have relationships with particular vendors at their farmers markets, source their groceries mostly at Whole Foods for organic and local, and supplement with Trader Joe's where appropriate. They both choose to buy and eat grass-fed, hormone free, free-range meat and have difficulties handling it at home. While Heather takes the time to plan, Brooke describes herself as an interesting mix of being disorganized with it always coming together

78 Michael Pollan, "Michael Pollan's Ideal Meal," interview by University of Minnesota Baaken Center for Spirituality & Healing, *Taking Charge of Your Health & Wellbeing*, YouTube, April 10, 2018, video, 2:58.

in the end. She's always searching for balance. It's all about the ebb and flow. Ideally, they (her family) would all eat the same thing, but they aren't at that point yet because of the toddlers. When they go to the farmers market on Sunday, Brooke's not really thinking of the meal—just the components of what to eat throughout the week. The balance is to think about what you eat in a week instead of daily, so she doesn't stress out about following the USDA-governed meal plate. It needs to be balanced over the course of the week, especially so the kids get their vegetables. A healthy system means everything in moderation.

Heather acknowledges that we spend a lot of time thinking about what we're going to eat. Not everyone is as conscientious. She wants to be wholesome and creative and spends much of her week thinking about meals and preparing for her family. She mentioned the statement that was popularized online recently, "Who knew the hardest part of being an adult was going to be figuring out what you're going to have for dinner every night of the week?" What is reiterated from Brooke earlier is the word "survival"—especially for families with toddlers and younger. What used to be enjoyed is now a task—or maybe a game—of nutrients. Finding the how, what, when, why mentioned earlier of creating healthy food (that will be eaten) for the child when there are so many options and opinions. And, just getting something on the plate, trying not to forget to feed yourself first.

TAKEAWAYS:

- Whether you are an accomplished author already aware of how to be responsible with your food choices, or you are meal prepping and trying to be creative with making healthy food for yourself and your family, you can acknowledge the overwhelming nature of our food system.

- When you think of the four components of your favorite meal, hear the stories of the other meals, and learn what brings the magic, you are in control.
- Think about the philosophy of food discussed by The Storytellers. Think about where it all begins.
- Think about how delicious your meal can be surrounded by those you love (and who love you), without staring at or listening to gadgets, made with seasonal ingredients sourced from local, organic, ethically raised farms, cooked by you. Yum!

CHAPTER 4:

CHOOSING ORGANIC OR NOT

———

Food is a blessing, and, if we eat carefully and consciously, we can transmute that input into an output of positive action, honest living, clear thinking, and love.

—ANNEMARIE COLBIN, PHD; FOOD THERAPIST, AUTHOR, QUALITY OF LIFE SUPERHERO

Organic adjective
or·gan·ic | \ ór-'ga-nik

Definition, per Merriam Webster: of, relating to, yielding, or involving the use of food produced with the use of feed or fertilizer of plant or animal origin without employment of chemically formulated fertilizers, growth stimulants, antibiotics, or pesticides.[79]

---

79   *Merriam-Webster*, s.v. "Organic," accessed May 26, 2020.

Before the year 1990, people used the term "organic" freely across farms and ranches to describe practices just as defined above without much worry that others were stating their products were organic when, in actuality, they were not. But, as is with most groups composed of human beings, there are those who do not tell the whole truth, either for their own gain or in ignorance of the consequences.

Therefore, the Organic Foods Production Act, part of the 1990 Farm Bill, was written to establish the National Organic Program (enacted by Congress in 2001), which is regulated by the Agricultural Marketing Service (AMS) of the United States Department of Agriculture.[80] The program, shaped by the already established Oregon Tilth, defined standard practices to oversee and ensure all operations follow specific guidelines. The operation, wishing to be organic, must first become certified and then agree to use the National List of Allowed Synthetic and Prohibited Non-Synthetic Substances, or "acceptable organic production inputs."[81, 82] Despite it being a national program, each state is allowed to adopt additional requirements approved by the USDA.

If not certified, it is illegal to use the word "organic" to define your product, unless you are a farm or ranch that grosses under $5,000 per year. These producers still need to abide by USDA regulations for growing but do not need to submit

80   "Organic Production/Organic Food: Information Access Tools," National Agricultural Library, USDA, accessed May 17, 2020.

81   "Transforming Farming and Food: Through Sustainable and Rigorous Standards," Certification, Oregon Tilth, accessed June 2, 2020.

82   "The National List," Agricultural Marketing Service, USDA, accessed June 1, 2020.

an organic systems plan to the certification program. The certification program is quite strict and involves a transition period of three years, during which there will be no application of prohibited substances (synthetic or non-synthetic substances that contribute to contamination of crops, soil, or water, as per the aforementioned National List).[83] These are the five basic steps to certification:[84]

1. The farm/business adopts organic practices, selects a USDA-accredited certifying agent, and submits an application and fees to the certifying agent.
   a. There are almost eighty certifying agents who work directly with the grower—the USDA just oversees.[85]
   b. Fees: a few hundred to several thousand dollars based on the certifying agent and the size, type, and complexity of the operation.
2. The certifying agent reviews the application to verify compliance with USDA organic regulations.
3. On-site inspection.
4. The certifying agent reviews the application and the inspector's report to determine the applicant's compliance with USDA organic regulations.
5. The certifying agent issues the organic certificate.
   a. To maintain certification, the applicant will go through an annual review and inspection process.

---

83 "What is Organic Certification?" National Organic Program, Agricultural Marketing Service, USDA, last modified June 2012.

84 Ibid.

85 "Certifier Locator," Organic Integrity Database, United States Department of Agriculture, Agricultural Marketing Service, accessed June 2, 2020.

STANDARDS/REGULATIONS

According to the Organic Trade Association, organic food sales in the US totaled approximately $47.9 billion in 2018, an increase of $2.7 billion from 2017.[86] Overall, organic products accounted for 6 percent of total food sales in 2018.[87] There has been a rise of organics ever since the AMS established the national program in 2002. I appreciate the standards established to maintain organic practices and the fact that every producer is reevaluated annually. It keeps farmers, either big or small producers, who want to commit fraud and pull the wool over the consumer's eyes at bay. There are three different areas of standards: 1) crop, 2) livestock, and 3) processing, labeling, and packaging. The USDA outlines them as follows:[88]

- **Crop Production**
  - As mentioned earlier, the land must have had no prohibited substances applied to it for at least three years before the harvest of an organic crop.
  - Soil fertility and crop nutrients will be managed through tillage and cultivation practices, crop rotations, and cover crops, supplemented with animal and crop waste materials, and allowed synthetic materials (per the National List).

---

86 Maggie McNeil, "US organic sales break through $50 billion mark in 2018: Sales hit a record $52.5 billion as organic becomes mainstream, says Organic Trade Association survey," Press Release, Organic Trade Association, May 17, 2019.

87 Ibid.

88 "Introduction to Organic Practices," USDA National Organic Program, Agricultural Marketing Service, last modified September 2015.

- Crop pests, weeds, and diseases will be controlled primarily through management practices including physical, mechanical, and biological controls. When these practices are not sufficient, an approved biological, botanical, or synthetic substance may be used (per the National List).
- Operations must use organic seeds and other planting stock when available.
- The use of genetic engineering, ionizing radiation, and sewage sludge is prohibited.

- **Livestock**
  - Livestock standards apply to animals used for meat, milk, eggs, and other animal products sold, labeled, or represented as organic. Some requirements include:
    - Animals for slaughter must be raised under organic management from the last third of gestation or, for poultry, no later than the second day of life.
    - Producers must feed livestock agricultural feed products that are 100 percent organic; they may also provide allowed vitamin and mineral supplements.
    - Dairy animals must be managed organically for at least twelve months in order for milk/dairy products to be sold, labeled, or represented as organic.
    - *Preventive management practices must be used to keep animals healthy.* Producers may not withhold treatment from sick or injured animals.

However, animals treated with a prohibited substance may not be sold as organic.
- Ruminants (e.g. cattle, sheep, goats) must be out on pasture for the entire grazing season, which is at least 120 days. These animals must also receive at least 30 percent of their intake from pasture.
- All organic livestock are required to have access to the outdoors year-round. Animals may only be temporarily confined due to documented environmental or health considerations.
- Organically raised animals must not be given hormones to promote growth or antibiotics for any reason.

- **Handling and Labeling** = selling, processing and packaging
  - *Handling*
    - All non-agricultural ingredients, whether synthetic or non-synthetic, must be included on the National List.
    - In a multi-ingredient product labeled as "organic," all agricultural ingredients must be organically produced, unless the ingredient(s) is not commercially available in organic form or allowed from the National List.
    - Handlers must prevent the co-mingling of organic and non-organic products and protect organic products from contact with prohibited substances.
  - *Labeling*
    - There are four distinct labeling categories for organic products:

- "One hundred percent organic"
  Products must be made up of 100 percent certified organic ingredients. The label must include the name of the certifying agent, e.g. Oregon Tilth, and may include the USDA Organic Seal and/or the 100 percent organic claim.

- "Organic"
  The product and ingredients must be certified organic, except where specified on the National List. Non-organic ingredients allowed per the National List may be used, but no more than 5 percent of the combined total ingredients may contain non-organic content. Additionally, the label must include the name of the certifying agent and may include the USDA Organic Seal and/or the organic claim.

- "'Made with' organic ingredients"
  At least 70 percent of the product must be certified organic ingredients. The organic seal **cannot** be used on the product and the final product cannot be represented as organic, with a maximum of three ingredients or ingredient categories represented as organic. Any remaining ingredients are not required to be organically produced but must be produced without genetic engineering. All non-agricultural products must be allowed on the National List, like enzymes in yogurt.

- "Specific organic ingredients"
  Multi-ingredient products with less than 70 percent certified organic content do not need to be certified. These products cannot display the USDA organic seal or use the word "organic" on the principal display panel.

They **can** list certified organic ingredients in the ingredient list and the percentage of organic ingredients.

———

- **Oregon Tilth**
  - Inspired in 1974 by Wendell Berry's words, "If we allow another generation to pass without doing what is necessary to enhance and embolden the possibility of strong agricultural communities, we will lose it altogether."[89]
  - Assisted in shaping and follows the standards of USDA National Organic Program.
  - An organic certifier—has direct interaction with growers/producers.
  - Over 1,800 members, from farmers to supermarkets, including producers of textiles and personal care products; domestic and international.[90]

BENEFITS?

So, now that you understand the certification process and labeling structure mandated by the AMS/USDA, let's discuss the benefits—or lack thereof—of eating organically. In general, organic produce is higher in antioxidants, vitamins, minerals, and flavonoids because of the increased fertility

———

89 Wendell Berry, "Agriculture for a Small Planet," symposium, Spokane,WA, 1974.

90 "People Like You: A community coming together to strengthen our food," Membership, Oregon Tilth, accessed June 2, 2020.

and quality of the soil, with special thanks to crop rotation.[91] Organically grown animals are healthier because they are devoid of synthetic antibiotics. Allergists and endocrinologists have stated that people who eat more organic produce develop less allergies and are less likely to become obese than those who eat non-organic produce.[92] By supporting organic producers, you are taking a stand (usually) for improved soil health, better land practices with decreased erosion and run off, and improved health of the surrounding flora, fauna, and humans. This, of course, depends on the farming/ranching practices.

We all know that conventional producers use synthetic chemicals—mostly harmful to the environment and humans when used in large quantities—for pesticides, insecticides, and fungicides. Despite pesticide residue on most produce being established as "safe" by the Environmental Protection Agency (EPA), why would you want to risk it?[93]

But, those who buy mostly organic are under the impression that produce is pesticide-free. I was recently having a conversation with my husband at dinner, discussing this chapter. When I mentioned organic pesticides, he asked, "Isn't that an oxymoron?" As a matter of fact, no, it is not. The problem

91 Marcin Barański et al., "Higher Antioxidant and Lower Cadmium Concentrations and Lower Incidence of Pesticide Residues in Organically Grown Crops: a Systematic Literature Review and Meta-Analyses," *British Journal of Nutrition* 112, no. 5 (July 2015): 794.

92 Axel Mie et al. "Human health implications of organic food and organic agriculture: a comprehensive review," *Environmental health: a global access science source* 16, no.1 (October 2017): 111.

93 "Food and Pesticides," United States Environmental Protection Agency, accessed May 26, 2020.

is that some scientists state that the compounds in organic pesticides are just as harmful as those found on regular produce.[94] Just because they are made in nature does not mean they are not toxic. It boils down to use rate, amount, and the common ingredients. Remember: -cide = killer.

As a consumer, you are trusting that the farmer has used the pesticide/insecticide/fungicide according to its label directions, whether you are buying organic or not.

Fortunately, the majority of our food is safe. The EPA allows only a very small percentage of the toxicity level in parts per million of the pesticide in order to ensure our safety. Any diet high in fruits and vegetables is best. I imagine there are more toxins in our environment and homes than in our food. Even the Environmental Working Group (EWG), who puts out the Dirty Dozen list (see below), states, "The health benefits of eating a diet rich in fruits and vegetables outweigh the risks of pesticide exposure. . . . Eating conventionally grown produce is far better than skipping fruits and vegetables."[95]

But I believe the benefits of eating organically grown food are greater overall.

For the most part, organic food costs more. This is because of the increased time it takes to develop and maintain healthy soil without any prohibited substances and the extra

---

94 Maureen Langlois, "Organic Pesticides: Not An Oxymoron," *Shots, Health News from NPR*, NPR, June 17, 2011.

95 "Should we eat more fruits and vegetables? What about the pesticide residue?" Frequently Asked Questions about Produce and Pesticides, Environmental Working Group, accessed May 26, 2020.

measures taken to ensure the product(s) remains organic. It costs more to produce the same amount of conventionally grown food because less is produced (due to the prohibited use of chemicals) per harvest. The higher cost is transferred to the consumer. Read on to find out how to choose organic while not breaking the bank.

IF YOU'RE ON THE FENCE . . .

The Dirty Dozen (no, not the 1967 WWII movie) is a list of fruits and vegetables released every year by the EWG that uses the data of the AMS/USDA's Pesticide Data Program (PDP) which "manages the sampling, testing, and reporting of pesticide residues on a wide variety of domestic and imported foods using a sound statistical program."[96, 97, 98] It is available to the general public and focuses on foods most consumed by children. Roughly ten thousand samples are collected and tested each year to determine which products retain the highest levels of pesticide residue, sometimes exceeding the amount the EPA allows. It rotates so it's never the same group, though many products make the list year after year.

You want to buy food with the least amount of pesticide residue to a) support your health, b) support your family's health,

---

96 *The Dirty Dozen*, directed by Robert Aldrch, written by Nunnally Johnson, Lukas Heller, and E.M. Nathanson (1967; Beverly Hills, CA: Metro-Goldwyn-Mayer Studios Inc.), film.

97 "Dirty Dozen," EWG's 2020 Shopper's Guide to Pesticides in Produceä, Environmental Working Group, accessed May 26, 2020.

98 "Pesticide Data Program," Agricultural Marketing Service, USDA, accessed May 26, 2020.

and c) feel good about your food choices. Here is your guide. **Always** buy these organic:

1. Strawberries
2. Spinach
3. Kale
4. Nectarines
5. Apples
6. Grapes*—very important. Raisins were the dirtiest commodity tested by the USDA, including organic. Don't let your kids or your loved ones eat packaged raisins. You can always get a dehydrator and make them yourself from cleaned organic grapes.
7. Peaches
8. Cherries
9. Pears
10. Tomatoes
11. Celery
12. Potatoes

Also using the PDP figures, the EWG lists the foods that include the least amount of pesticides, known as the Clean Fifteen.[99] The EWG stated that 70 percent of these fifteen foods presented no detectable pesticide residue. Show me those samples and where they came from so I can go there! (Liz Lemon, anyone?)[100] You can be okay with buying these from a conventional farmer at the farm stand/market or if there is no organic section in your local supermarket:

99 "Clean Fifteen," EWG's 2020 Shopper's Guide to Pesticides in Produceä, Environmental Working Group, accessed May 26, 2020.

100 "Liz Lemon," *30 Rock*, portrayed and created by Tina Fey (2006-2013; New York, NY: National Broadcasting Company), series, television.

13. Avocados
14. Sweet corn
15. Pineapples
16. Frozen sweet peas
17. Onions
18. Papayas
19. Eggplants
20. Asparagus
21. Kiwis
22. Cabbages
23. Cauliflower
24. Cantaloupes
25. Broccoli
26. Mushrooms
27. Honeydew melons

Per the EWG, "All research agrees on the health benefits of a diet that includes fruits and vegetables, and eating fresh produce—organic or conventional, as budget allows—is essential for health."[101] Don't be scared by pesticide residue because, luckily, there are safeguards in place to monitor abuses and overexposure. This brings me to . . .

APPLES AND ORANGES

Let's turn our attention to apples and oranges. My older brother told me a story about the Cosmic Crisp apple. He lives in Lake Stevens, Washington, and had never had this brand of apple before moving there. That's because it's grown

---

101 EWG's 2019 Shopper's Guide to Pesticides in Produceä, Environmental Working Group, accessed February 16, 2020.

in Washington State and sold in Washington State (and, as its website states, all over the country—but not guaranteed).[102] It was brought to his attention in its home state, where it is grown and bred locally. It has gone through over twenty years of development and non-GMO breeding through a collaboration with a horticulturist, the Washington State University's fruit tree breeding program, and a pome fruit breeder.[103] It is a cross between the Enterprise and Honeycrisp and named for the starburst-like formations on its skin. David claims it is one of the best apples he's ever had.

On to the next apple story. My friend Bucky and her husband were lamenting recently about missing New York City's Union Square farmers market and how she misses the apples. There was always at least one vendor who had the Winesap variety, originally grown in Virginia and New Jersey. "And they were wonderful," stated Bucky. She could always get them. (I cannot buy them in California. When we were in Rochester, New York, over the holidays, I found some at the local farm stand. They *really* are wonderful.) Now that she lives in Missouri, Bucky cannot find anything that is not a typical regular version at the market these days. Growing up outside of Kansas City, every year they would go pick four or five bushels—"Such fun memories every year growing up!"—from Stephenson's apple orchard, a fourth-generation, small-production local orchard of apples and peaches with its own restaurant, store, and cider mill. "There were a lot of Jonathan, just straight Jonathan apples, which are kind

---

102 "Where to Buy Apples," Learn, Cosmic Crispâ, accessed May 26, 2020.

103 "History," Flavor, Cosmic Crispâ, accessed May 26, 2020.

of like a flavor of a Macintosh but not as soft and mushy. . . . great to bake with."

But you cannot go pick them now. You can go buy them at the store, but you cannot pick them yourself at the orchard. She told me that around the year 2000, the orchard stopped allowing u-pick because volume and traffic became unsustainable. She surmised that it was a small family business with aging owners who experienced difficulty adapting to new business models as agriculture evolved to become "bigger" and "faster." In 2007, the restaurant closed. And now, unfortunately, there is a QuikTrip in its place.[104]

Let's end this discussion with the Cara Cara Navel orange. There is little that gets me excited for winter more than the Cara Cara orange. It is a mutation from a Washington navel grown in Venezuela, discovered in the 1970s.[105] It was available to specialty markets for a while from November to April and shipped from South America. I found them at Fairway Market in New York City and, one day, spent $18 on a bag of them. It was oranges in winter in New York City. Of course they were expensive. I thought I would never see the Cara Cara again once I moved away. Fairway Market had really good buyers and sold not-so-typical items that you would not normally find at Shop Rite or C-Town markets. Lo and behold, during my first winter in Santa Barbara, I found them at Sprouts. And they were grown in California. No buyer's remorse for buying oranges from South America!

---

104 Adrianne DeWeese, "Stephenson's old location to become QuikTrip," *The Examiner,* June 29, 2011.

105 "What is the difference between Navel Oranges and Cara Cara Oranges?" Fruit facts, Hale Groves, September 4, 2018.

(I told you this book is just as important for me as it is for you.) And the best news is, I can now find them at our local farmers market and supermarket into late spring.

LOCAL

So, apples and oranges. What's important is finding what tastes good that is close to you. It is your choice where you buy from, whether it's CVS or the farmers market. Nowadays, the huge markets and highly efficient, centralized distribution centers have allowed almost all products to enter the food supply without much connection to what is surrounding you at the local level. Look for the "Local" symbol or sticker on products where you shop. Better yet, go talk to your farmers if you have access to a farm stand or farmers market. Whether it be berries off the vine in early summer or your other favorite fruit, think of where it came from and who is producing it. Unfortunately, Bucky cannot find the same Jonathan apples from thirty years ago and she does not have as much access to local farm stands as she did in NYC. So, she makes different choices and determines what she can get that tastes good, from her region, throughout the year.

My brother, Paul, told me a story of a conventional berry farmer. It was in the early summer, and Paul had the chance to talk with the farmer as he purchased produce for the farm stand's CSA boxes. The farmer said they would choose a locally grown farm-fresh berry over a flown-in organically grown berry any day of the week. What they meant by "farm fresh" was "straight off the vine." Even though that crop might have been sprayed with something, it was grown, there, outside with the sun. And, the farmer knew where it was grown because it was *their* farm.

Paul stated that, to this day, it's a little hard for him to understand. He also admitted he didn't have a lot of exposure to how differently things taste when fresh off the vine versus bought in the supermarket. But as far as walking with the farmer on the farm, the farmer's statement puzzled Paul. He said, "We spend so much time hearing about how bad pesticides are, specifically involving the monoculture aspect of agriculture in this country. It is really negative, and so that really sticks out in my mind, because the farmer said they would eat that berry, even though it was grown with pesticide sprayed on it, because it tastes so much better when it's fresh."

GROUNDED
This takes me back to my original premise: making the best choice for yourself, the environment, and the animals, in order for you to be healthful and eat good food. This *also* brings in the debate of buying organic blueberries from Peru in December when a) it's not blueberry season and b) you're paying a lot of money for something that has traveled a very long way. Obviously, it is your choice. But in this self-help guide I want to inform—no, *empower* you, to connect more to the land around you. If you can eat locally *and* organically, that's like winning the lottery. There are many farmers who cannot nor will not pay for the organic certification, but they still adhere to USDA regulations. And they produce delicious, truly "organic" food.

The moral of the story: buy local. There is *nothing* wrong with choosing all organic. Most of the time, the small production farms use traditional organic methods anyway. But, when in doubt, ask!

TAKEAWAYS:

- A lot goes into obtaining and maintaining organic certification.
- The "Organic" label neither means small production nor pesticide-free. But, in general, it is cleaner, and there are more rules associated with maintaining the quality of organically grown food.
- Our biggest concern is with the twelve items on the Dirty Dozen. Always buy those organic (if you have the means and accessibility). And watch out for raisins! If they were included in the list, they would be number one and not just a side note.
- If you cannot afford to buy, or don't have access to, organically grown food, at least maintain a diet rich in fruits and vegetables, even if grown conventionally. The EPA keeps us safe with its research on pesticides regarding how much humans can ingest before it becomes toxic. Wash your produce when you bring it home from the market or farm stand. Or grow your own (with the least amount of synthetic pesticides, of course).
- What I enjoy about eating locally is supporting and meeting the producers, talking to them, and asking questions about the "fruits" of their labor (pun intended).

CHAPTER 5:

SOIL

——

Where does your food come from? Is it coming from soil that has life growing in it? If you cannot confidently answer this question, you might want to ask yourself why you do not believe you are worthy. Because you are worthy. . . . You are worth food and nourishment that is raised on soil with life giving force."

—NITI BALI; FARM TO FORK RIOT FOUNDER, AUTHOR, ANOTHER GENUINE BAD ASS

I have a black thumb. It is unfortunate because I love watching plants grow. "Moderate moist with indirect light" does not seem that difficult, right? I just don't have the knack, or really, the practice. Luckily, others do. I'd love to grow my own food.

Speaking of, have you watched the documentary, *The Biggest Little Farm*?[106] I believe it is one of the most important

---

106 *The Biggest Little Farm*, directed by John Chester, written by John Chester and Mark Monroe (2018; Los Angeles, CA: Diamond Docs, FarmLore Films), documentary.

stories. Ever. It is the story of soil. And I imagine it represents the experience of many new farmers: buying or taking over dead dry rocky dirt and transforming it into healthy, viable soil to support hundreds of species. Wendell Berry, author and environmental activist, stated in his collection of essays *Bringing it to the Table*, "most people nowadays lack even a superficial knowledge of agriculture, and most who do know something about it are paying little or no attention to what is happening under the surface."[107] Therefore, watching the documentary opened my eyes to what is required to build a farm one microbe at a time, and now I know what is happening under the surface.

I want *you* to know what is happening under the surface and why it is so important for the quality of not only your food, but your life. This next part of the book includes some basics that every food listener needs to know, including information on soil health, the beef industry, and other alternatives in order to make healthy choices for your favorite meal. I am biased toward regenerative agriculture, but I believe in eating fruits and vegetables. And so, I don't want you to feel like I'm ganging up on big agriculture. I believe when nature is manipulated too much, things backfire.

First, let us take a walk down memory lane to high school biology class, shall we? The circle of human life revolves around oxygen and nitrogen. If we don't get either, we're dead. Luckily for us, our planet's air contains both oxygen and nitrogen. We exhale nitrogen, oxygen, and carbon dioxide.

107 Wendell Berry, *Bringing It to the Table: On Farming and Food* (Berkeley: Counterpoint, 2009), 173.

As for plants, once a plant's chlorophyll traps the sunlight, it absorbs carbon dioxide. Water from the soil is sucked up through the plant's roots and combines with the carbon dioxide to begin the photosynthesis process, which first splits the hydrogen and oxygen of the water. Oxygen is released into the atmosphere; then, hydrogen combines with carbon dioxide to make glucose, which the plant uses and stores for growth and energy. The plant will pass that energy along to the organisms that eat it. The sugars enrich the soil through the roots. Both living and decomposing plants feed the soil by increasing the amount of nutrient-rich organic matter, which is integral to the cycle of the plant and its continued health. Without those nutrients, the plant will die.

This nutrient-rich organic matter is the result of building soil successfully. It involves the fluid balance of bacteria, earthworms, minerals, and dirt with water. All of which were void when John and Molly Chester, determined to farm and transform their land, arrived at the Moorpark, California, property that would eventually become Apricot Lane Farms, featured in *The Biggest Little Farm*.[108] The 200 acre parcel was almost uninhabitable. Monocrop farming practices—choosing one crop to plant on the same soil every year (typically corn, soy, or wheat) usually accompanied by tilling and regular use of pesticides—had left destroyed land of lost topsoil, erosion, pollution, and significant water run-off with every rainstorm. Luckily, their investors were patiently stoic while waiting for the Chesters to produce soil, compost, and be the catalysts for a working profitable farm.

---

108 *The Biggest Little Farm*, directed by John Chester, written by John Chester and Mark Monroe (2018; Los Angeles, CA: Diamond Docs, FarmLore Films), documentary.

With help from Alan York, an expert in biodynamics, they designed a farm that included a very diverse mix of crops and animals to work in concert in order to rebuild the soil. "Between year five and seven, we saw such an immense return of biodiversity that we became aware of nature's intent to balance out epidemics of pest and disease that we'd been struggling with years prior. That was like the cavalry coming over the hill in the third act of the film when you thought that the cavalry would never show up. It was that profound and splendid," said John Chester. Apricot Lane Farms is now certified organic, provides product to multiple farmers markets, and host tours at the farm. It was, and continues to be, a remarkable transformation and a demonstration of patience, time, science, art, and dedication.

MONOCROPPING AND SOME HISTORY

Folks, let us not forget the Dust Bowl, the *Super-Size Me* version of monocrop farming practices that devastated the land and lives of thousands of Americans last century. It is the complete opposite of what the Chesters accomplished. Mind you, the Chesters bought land in California that was already tilled and over-plowed to the point of erosion *and* had the opportunity to learn from mistakes of all who came before them. The area of the great plains was brand new territory, all for the taking.

I understand what happened. We humans run toward anything that is abundant and relatively "free." (I see you, open bar). And we are very good at assuming whatever it is will be there for eternity without considering the consequences of our actions. Hence, the practice of the pioneers living up to their idea of manifest destiny. The plains across the United States—including land in Texas, New Mexico, Colorado, Kansas, and Oklahoma—presented acres and acres of grasslands available to those moving west after the Civil War and assisted by the government granting land use and other acts for homesteading. During the first two decades of the 1900s, inexperienced farmers cultivated row crops like wheat and corn on semi-arid land with little to no irrigation supply, over-plowing, and limited knowledge about regeneration or soil health.

A quartet of events—increased demand for wheat from Europe, use of new gasoline-powered farming equipment, the stock market crash in 1929, and the beginning of what would be an almost decade-long drought—caused absolute destruction and devastation for farmers and those living throughout the region. Wheat prices fell. No money or subsidies were available. Any nutrients that had once preserved the health of the grasses and helped to fix the soil were not replenished.

There were no roots to hold it all down, and in 1932, the dust storms began. The dust covered 300,000 square miles from mid-Texas, west to New Mexico, east to the eastern borders of Oklahoma and Kansas, north through Colorado and Nebraska to Montana, Wyoming, and South Dakota. The storms continued through 1938, reaching all the way to Manhattan.[109] Wind eroded the crops, and locusts and rabbits took what was left. Roughly six thousand five hundred people died, either from dust pneumonia or fleeing cross-country to a better life.

---

109 "Dust Bowl," History, updated February 21, 2020.

After having initially advertised the plains as grand for opportunity, the government, now under President Franklin Delano Roosevelt, stepped in with multiple groups to assist the farmers. Most importantly, FDR formed the Soil Erosion Service, later named the Soil Conservation Service and now known as the Natural Resources Conservation Service, in order to restore the region's soil health and to encourage regenerative approaches, like planting native grasses to redevelop the root system and increase the soil organic matter—the "hodgepodge" I mention later.[110] He mandated the planting of two hundred million trees from Texas to Canada to create a wind break and to decrease the effects of blowing dust. He paid farmers, who were reluctant to practice different techniques, one dollar per acre of land. He was adamant about revitalizing the devastated plains in order to get America's farmers back on their feet again. In his Fireside Chat in September 1936, he commented on the drought and the dust bowl after he had visited the plains.[111]

---

110 David Woolner, "FDR and the New Deal Response to an Environmental Catastrophe," *Energy & Environment, Franklin & Eleanor* (blog), *Roosevelt Institute*, June 3, 2010.

111 President (1933-1945: Roosevelt). 1933-1945. Fireside Chat on Drought Conditions. 1936-09-06. Retrieved from the Digital Public Library of America, accessed January 19, 2020.

"No cracked earth, no blistering sun, no burning wind, no grasshoppers, are a permanent match for the indomitable American farmers and stockmen and their wives and children who have carried on through desperate days, and inspire us with their self-reliance, their tenacity and their courage. It was their fathers' task to make homes; it is their task to keep those homes; it is our task to help them with their fight."

— FRANKLIN DELANO ROOSEVELT

Thankfully, those systems put into place in the 1930s enabled the land to heal. As the United States grew, people moved away from the farms, further west and into cities. The 1950s and '60s allowed for the farmers to glean more experience and teach their families proper practices for land management. Farmers formulated better crops and more effective pesticides, which improved overall yield. Livestock took over as the largest consumer of row crops, specifically grain. Grain was the largest export during the 1970s, raising food and farm prices.[112] In order to handle the demand, President Nixon's administration encouraged farmers to plant "fence

---

112 May Peters et al., "Agricultural Commodity Prices Spikes in the 1970s and 1990s: Valuable Lessons for Today," *Amber Waves,* Economic Research Service, USDA, March 1, 2009.

row to fence row" and advocated for larger production farms, which were deemed more profitable.

Fast forward almost fifty years later. With the continued revolution of industry, perpetuating faster with more efficient machinery, along with chemical fertilizers and pesticides, the soil continues to be under attack. Ironically, there is discussion that if the mega-farmers do not change their practices, if Earth's temperatures continue to rise and catastrophic environmental events become more frequent, a second Dust Bowl could occur.[113] As water sources are depleting, it might already be starting, and despite it not being of the same scale as last century's, it could still cause mass devastation.

My point for this information is for you to understand that we can—and should—prevent history from repeating itself.

The soil degradation across North America over the last forty years is substantial. It's becoming harder to maintain a good level of hodgepodge. Dr. Allen Williams, a cattle rancher in Mississippi, travels around the world consulting farmers/ranchers on restoring soil health. He focuses on restoring soil health for improved water retention, reduced runoff, increased land productivity, enhanced plant and wildlife

---

113 "Desertification," Special Report: Special Report on Climate Change and Land, Intergovernmental Panel on Climate Change, accessed May 21, 2020.

biodiversity, and healthier food.[114] Per his research, soil erosion and degradation have caused the abandonment of 430 million hectares (a hectare is equivalent to 100 acres). This equals one-third of all present cropland.[115] Even though FDR put those measures in place for the land to regenerate, Dr. Williams says the soil erosion was irreparable. So, we should just give up now, right? Nope. Keep reading!

The final piece of this history is Dr. Williams' story of a massive dust storm in Eastern Colorado/Western Kansas in January 2018(!). A dust storm in the middle of winter. So strange! And, later in 2018, he experienced hurricane-force winds while driving to the airport in Oklahoma. Red dust blew for the entire forty-mile drive. At one point, he had to slow down to thirty miles per hour for safety. By the time he arrived in Oklahoma City, the entire city was blanketed in a red haze.[116] This amount of choking dust causes hypoxia (decreased oxygen) in people, on land and in water. He stated that, because of the extreme wind events in 2018, fishermen lost billions of dollars of revenue due to the dust magnifying the existing dead zone in the Gulf of Mexico.[117]

- **Dead zone:** an area of ocean or larger lake with excessively low levels of oxygen due to polluted nutrient run-off from

---

114 "Dr. Allen Williams, Ph.D.," Chief Ranching Officer at Joyce Farms, Joyce Farms, accessed May 21, 2020.

115 "Allen Williams—Restore Soil and Ecosystem Health with Adaptive Grazing," Quiriva Conference, *Ranching and Farming at the Radical Center,* filmed by Crash Roll Films, Albuquerque, NM., November 15-17, 2017, YouTube video, 4:23.

116 Ibid., 8:29.

117 Ibid., 8:50.

farms or water treatment plants upstream.[118] Aquatic life dies. Algae tends to grow, absorbing the remaining oxygen, and cutting off the sun's ability to reach below the water's surface, causing further death.

- The largest dead zone in the United States is about 6,500 square miles in the Gulf of Mexico. It is a result of nutrient pollution from the Mississippi River Basin, especially bad every summer due to summertime harvest.[119]

  – To recap: With the same effect as the 1930s, wind erosion diminished the integrity of the already-stressed infrastructure of root systems due to over-tilling of what was treated as topsoil. Combined with significant use of pesticides, there was nothing to hold the organic matter in place. Once it started to rain in Oklahoma and its surrounding region, the run-off—including the red dust mixed with fertilizers from the farms and substandard land and water filtration systems—entered water sources that flowed into the Gulf, killing marine life.

  – This occurrence is an unfortunate unintended consequence of poor soil health.

RIGHTEOUS REGENERATIVE AGRICULTURE

What I know to be important and to prevent another Dust Bowl is what many farmers are adopting these days: regenerative agricultural practices that focus on crop rotation like nature intended. Some farmers have been doing this from

---

118 *Merriam-Webster*, s.v. "dead zone," accessed May 21, 2020.

119 "The Effects: Dead Zones and Harmful Algae Blooms," Nutrient Pollution, United States Environmental Protection Agency, accessed May 21, 2020.

the beginning. This is "beyond organic." Remember farmer Joel Salatin? This includes rotational cash crops with cover crops and holistic grazing to ensure healthy soil and to preserve what's "under the surface." These practices equal the righteous way to produce food.

Let's revisit Salatin's idea that there are two ways to produce food, and you can choose what you want to support. Unrighteous means behavior that is disrespectful toward our animal stewards, prompting poor health for animals, land, and consumers.

Righteous means one that ultimately heals with food; it takes care of the bodies of the consumers, considers earthworm health and population, builds soil, maintains the hydrologic cycle of water, and retains raindrops (decreased topsoil loss with run-off). The soil built is a dark rich brown, like chocolate cake, that smells fresh, displays a hodgepodge of earthworms, fungi, and other micro/bacteria. When touched, it coats your hands with reserved water molecules. That hodgepodge is needed to aerate the soil and create avenues for nutrients and water to move through to supply the plants and support growth.

The earthworms also build organic matter by eating decaying plant material and littering the soil with castings that act as natural fertilizer. Per Sandra Keats, the producer of *The Biggest Little Farm*, "The worms eat what we feed them and poop it out," she said.[120]

---

120 Anne Thompson, "Why Breakout Documentary 'The Biggest Little Farm' Didn't Sell to Netflix, from Poop to Nuts," Indiewire, May 13, 2019.

"The worm castings are the gold of fertility. This is super-rich, dense worm poop. They have microbe-rich gut bacteria. As the worms eat the compost, their gut biology infuses it with more microorganisms. We take the worm poop and cut a two-inch layer off the bottom and put it in the brewer. Any time we're irrigating, we inject the brewed tea straight into our irrigation system and spread this all over the farm."

—KEATS

The farmers who have moved away from what we presently think of as "conventional"—focusing solely on yield, free use of chemicals, no focus on crop rotation or cover crops— to regenerative agriculture admit the upfront expenses including nutrient management and composting. Eventually, they demonstrate higher yields because each cycle creates healthier and healthier soil. These practices protected the groundwater with improved infiltration, decreased run-off and erosion that results in reduced overall water needs, and lowered overhead costs. In general, unfortunately, people believe that this way of farming is not sustainable enough to feed the world because of the amount of seed and resources required for each successful harvest. But cover crops bene-fiting the cash crops and feeding the soil with carbon is not an arbitrary outcome measure. The more carbon in the soil, the healthier the environment and the less amount of excess carbon dioxide emitted as a greenhouse gas. It seems so easy.

———

And yet, it's not.

Sir Albert Howard (1873-1947), often referred to as the father of organic agriculture, wrote *An Agricultural Testament* in 1940.[121] He was the first Westerner to document agricultural practices in India, which were significantly different from what was happening in America. He struggled with supporting America's conventional farming practices. He made the connection with healthy soil, humans, animal population, and crops. In *Testament*, he stated, "Natural methods of soil management must form the basis of all our studies of soil fertility."[122] It astounds me that he wrote the book in 1940 because it could have been written today.

———

121   Keith Addison, "Albert Howard," Journey to Forever, accessed May 17, 2020.

122   Sir Albert Howard, *An Agricultural Testament* (New York: Oxford University Press, 1943).

"The main characteristic of Nature's farming can therefore be summed up in a few words. Mother earth never attempts to farm without live stock; she always raises mixed crops; great pains are taken to preserve the soil and to prevent erosion; the mixed vegetable and animal wastes are converted into humus; there is no waste; the processes of growth and the processes of decay balance one another; ample provision is made to maintain large reserves of fertility; the greatest care is taken to store the rainfall; both plants and animals are left to protect themselves against disease."

—SIR ALBERT HOWARD

We are decreasingly connected to the health of the soil, understanding less and less that we are what we eat. "Healthy soil equals healthy food equals healthy people" is not necessarily a new concept, but it is one most people do not think about as they reach for their prepackaged salad or presorted carton of eggs or gallon of ice cream. "Once the demand for food and raw materials increases and good prices are obtained for the produce of the soil, the pressure on soil fertility becomes intense. The temptation to convert this fertility into money becomes irresistible," Howard wrote.

HOLISTIC PLANNED GRAZING—THE GURUS

The last piece of the soil health puzzle is livestock, most definitely included in Sir Howard's agricultural belief system. I am intrigued by the animal's place in the symbiotic, biodiverse relationship of maintaining adequate soil organic matter for prolonged maximal soil health to promote healthy successful cash crop yields. It includes planned grazing for cows, sheep, or goats on different pastures for one to two days at a time and moving them to another pasture for one to two days, allowing the previous pasture to recover (sometimes for months). The benefit is the aerated fertilized soil, which can be seeded—if need be—especially once the flock of chickens scratch through the dung and disseminate it over the land. This system is meant to mimic nature in keeping the herd together in small areas and moving them quickly to thwart attacks by predators.

This is the design of Allan Savory, the father of holistic management and planned grazing.[123] He acknowledges many people believe cows are destroying the planet. When you look closer, it is the poor management of cows that helps to destroy the planet (i.e. humans). Humans have forced animals meant to freely move around and compete for the best vegetation (while avoiding predators by staying close together) into excessive confinement at feed lots in metal crates, where they are force-fed unnatural ingredients and antibiotics or are let out to huge pastures where they eat the same flora daily with no plan. People *can* successfully manage the land and have been doing so for millennia. Farming practices that employ observing and responsibly listening to the land and animals succeed more often than not. (Here's lookin' at you, Dust Bowl.)

The evidence is the soil regenerated on dead land. The positive result occurs once the farmers/ranchers change their practices to focus on following, not defying, nature's lead. The evidence is the health of the products grown with the compost and earthworm poop and fortified by the nutrients catalyzed by photosynthesis. Therefore, by using livestock as the natural machines, Savory has sustained Sir Howard's vision of following nature's lead in maintaining healthy soil and regenerating dead acres. Savory stated, "As we know it, we have destroyed civilizations through agriculture, more than armies have ever done. And we're now facing a similar global situation. Livestock are the only thing that can save

123 "Our Mission," About Us, Savory Institute, accessed May 21, 2020.

us now."[124] Not in the sense that it provides meat, but in that it is the center of the cyclical natural tilling and fertilizing system to produce healthy land and soils to support more nutrient-dense crops with improved water infiltration.

There are three ranchers who followed Savory's techniques, named the Soil Carbon Cowboys: Dr. Allen Williams (mentioned earlier), Neil Dennis, and Gabe Brown.[125, 126] Dennis, in particular, was a good representative. He was part of the majority of his ranching community: skeptical to Savory's practices after learning to farm conventionally. He knew big equipment, commercial fertilizers and pesticides, pushing for yield instead of quality, focusing on his animals instead of the land. But after years of struggling due to drought and crop failure, the bank suggested he sell off a portion of his land but continue the same techniques. Without improvement, Dennis knew there had to be changes made, or else he'd have to go "flip hamburgers somewhere."

Per the nudging of his wife, Dennis attended a seminar on holistic management and spent the next six years determined to prove wrong what he was taught. He photographed two separate paddocks on his land in Saskatchewan, Canada. One was farmed with his traditional practices, and the other was managed holistically. He was unable to prove his education wrong because the holistic paddock produced better

124 Allan Savory, "How Livestock and Grassland Soils Can Save Civilization," Northern Plains Grasslands Symposium, filmed July 19, 2017, Bismarck, ND, YouTube video, 11:11.

125 "Soil Carbon Cowboys," Grass Fed Solutions: The Online Guide to Low-Cost Pasture-Based Cattle Farming, accessed October 7, 2019.

126 "Soil Carbon," carbon nation, accessed October 7, 2019.

yield, increased soil health, and improved water infiltration. He added his mom was not excited about all of the weeds but now the weeds are presented as a symptom of improved soil nutrients and are consumed by the cows, providing them more protein than some of the feed crops. "It's extremely low stress because we're working with nature instead of against it," said Dennis. The soil benefitted, as did his cows. His use of medicine for treating his cows was inversely related to his soil health and crop yield.

Gabe Brown in North Dakota also experienced crop failure due to drought and poor land/animal stewardship. He almost lost his 1,760-acre farm between 1995 and 1999 due to natural disasters, but he was determined to rebuild. Having lost almost everything and with no money to buy synthetic fertilizers and pesticides (i.e. the input), he was forced to implement holistic grazing with cover crop, polyculture practices. What happened was improved soil resilience and yield. He has not looked back.

To take things a step further, in 2006, Brown experimented with one-acre plots to gauge the difference, if any, of monoculture versus polyculture practices.[127] He used a variety of single row crops including radish, turnip, soybean, cowpea, and lupin, planting the last row with a cocktail mix of all of the monoculture seeds. The mix is usually planted as cover crops in between cash crops to fix nitrogen into the soil to absorb carbon and eliminate the need for fertilizers

---

127 Gabe Brown, "Keys to Building a Healthy Soil," *Holistic Regeneration of Our Lands: A Producer's Perspective,"* Idaho Center for Sustainable Agriculture's annual symposium, filmed by Transcend Productions, Boise, ID, November 18, 2014, YouTube video, 12:58.

and pesticides. It also provides excellent sources for the bees and other pollinators. Over the course of two months, the polyculture acre produced three times as much as the other plots, with very little rainfall.

Since 2015, Brown has stopped using synthetic fertilizer, and his ranch has grown to 5,000 acres.

"Why do I want to go out and spend thousands upon thousands of dollars every year on synthetic fertilizer when I can grow these crops for just the cost of the seed? They'll make the nitrogen for me and then my livestock will come around and eat these plants, then convert it to dollars for me. So I'm getting all my fertilizer basically for a profit because I'm making money off of these crops."

—GABE BROWN

THE DIRT

These examples of successful farming practices, attending to the land and mimicking nature, demonstrate the importance of soil management. So why is this important? As you have read, your life depends on it. And as I stated earlier:

healthy soil equals healthy crops equals healthy animals equals healthy humans.

Huge conventional farms have disrupted nature to focus on efficiency and profit. You might tell me that this, in a world where people are hungry, is not a bad thing. First off, the food produced needs to be distributed equitably, which does not happen. Secondly, there is a long-term environmental and human cost to bigger and faster. The earth cannot sustain these practices, and humans are suffering from increased disease and malnutrition.

There is an argument that a carrot today is not the same carrot our grandparents ate as children, due to the nutrient depletion of the soil from overuse of the land and focus on yield instead of quality.[128] This study showed that, as compared to 1950, in 1999 a carrot presented less calcium, more carbohydrates, less ash (a reflection of all minerals, primarily potassium), less iron, more phosphorus (which makes sense because phosphorus is a major element in fertilizer), more Vitamin A, and more thiamin.[129] But just because they might not be as rich in minerals as their ancestors, fruits and vegetables are still an integral part of a healthy diet. We just need to be more aware of where they come from and how they are grown. For instance, how often have you bought lettuce from the grocery store only to watch it turn brown in a matter of

---

128 "Dirt Poor: Have Fruits and Vegetables Become Less Nutritious?" Environment, Sustainability, *Scientific American,* April 27, 2011.

129 Donald R. Davis et al., "Changes in USDA Food Composition for 43 Garden Crops, 1950-1999," *Journal of the American College of Nutrition* 23, no. 6 (May 2004): 675.

hours? (I don't want lettuce that has been modified to last longer on the shelf—that's not natural).

Lettuce, sourced from sustainable farms that care about the soil health and that work the land with or without the help from animals, a) is more delicious, b) lasts longer because it comes from better nutrient stock, and c) is more healthful due to healthier nutrients in the soil. I have never heard of lettuce being recalled from a larger-production sustainable farm. Recently, there have been recalls of produce, specifically lettuces, due to toxic levels of E. coli traced back to huge mono crop farms, organic and conventional.[130] This is due to very poor land and water management.

TAKEAWAYS:
- We need to support a system of responsible stewards getting in touch with the land and protecting the animals in order to provide better produce with consistent nutrient sequestration and water infiltration.
- Thankfully, gurus like Sir Howard put in the time and research so the Chesters could transform a barren landscape into a flourishing multispecies organic farm. And Savory has developed a system of working the land that has benefitted farmers/ranchers around the world by using livestock correctly as part of the mutualistic relationship between the land, humans, and animals.
- These farmers and ranchers, who practice holistic and sustainable methods and regenerate their soils, are

---

130 "Outbreak Investigation of E. coli: Romaine from Salinas, California (November 2019)," *FDA publishes Investigation Report and shares key finding,* US Food & Drug Administration, May 21, 2020.

conscious of their consumers but also of their own health, producing higher quality products with better soil, thinking about their impact on the future. We need to support them to support the soil, now that you know what's happening under the surface.

- It is possible to sustain our food system with these practices. Plus, that is how your food will taste its best. You will be supporting a righteous way to food production. And a righteous way to live.

Rest in Peace, Neil Dennis.

CHAPTER 6:

BEEF

If you don't eat yer meat, you can't have any pudding! How can you have any pudding if you don't eat yer meat?

—ROGER WATERS; SERIOUS ROCKER, KEEPING UP WITH THE TIMES IN 1979

Beef. It's what's for dinner! When those commercials were released, I was taken more toward the music (Aaron Copland's "Hoedown" from *Rodeo*) than I was drooling over the slab of steak on the television screen. But it clearly made an impact because I still remember the commercials. And I am still eating beef.

Beef is not for everyone though. And nowadays, with the documentary *Gamechangers*, the National Foreign Press deciding to serve vegan fare at the 2020 Golden Globes, the Intergovernmental Panel on Climate Change's recent report—including its chapter on Food Security—and an upward trend in restaurants featuring seasonal vegetables, more people seem to be coming to terms with the overall impact of eating beef.[131] This chapter is not an expose on the meat/beef industry. There are multiple sources for that already written and produced. This is a discussion of what you can think about if you decide to buy beef.

I am the daughter of a vegetarian. I remember my mother stopped eating meat cold turkey—such a strange saying!—after cooking our Christmas roast beef in 2006. She states it was her reaction to watching a National Geographic documentary that featured a fisherman hoisting an innocent fish onto his boat and using a mallet to deliver the killing blow. It affected her tremendously. She claimed it grossed her out to put the roast onto the table and she did not enjoy or want to continue the tradition any longer. She has not had any taste of animal flesh since and has switched to non-cow's milk, but she will eat the occasional cheese. This was someone whose treat would be the occasional Filet-O-Fish sandwich, fries, and chocolate shake. I am proud of her dedication to creating a world for herself where she is doing her conscious part to protect animals.

I have participated in almost every type of diet: Paleo, Atkins, South Beach, Whole30, vegetarian, pescatarian, no sugar, blood type, spring-into-summer elimination—all with good results except for constantly craving donuts, chocolate ice cream, and French fries. Intermittent fasting has not made it into my routine due to the anxiety that accompanies the idea—just ask my husband how hangry I get. . . . I know, I know, it's a learning experience. Perhaps one day I'll

---

131 *Gamechangers,* directed by Louie Psihoyos, written by Shannon Kornelsen, Mark Monroe, and Joseph Pace (2018; ReFuel Productions, Oceanic Preservation Soceity, Diamond Docs), documentary.

incorporate it. But for now, I know what works for me. This is what I consider to be healthy: occasional red meat, mostly eggs, chicken and fish, rarely dairy, rarely bread or pasta or dessert, good quality oils, lots of fresh seasonal vegetables bought at our local farm stand.

THE INDUSTRY

I knew I would need to research the cattle industry, but I started with binge-geeking out on sustainable farmers first, procrastinating on the inevitable. I did think in the beginning, "Hmm, maybe I'll just have a plate of vegetables as my favorite meal. That should be easier." But, I knew I would be lying. I am very aware of the processes our large beef-growing and packing plants take to enhance efficiency in order to make profit. I am very aware of the environmental impact of just one pound of beef; it takes approximately 2,000 gallons of water, twelve pounds of grain, thirty-five pounds of topsoil, and the energy equivalent to one gallon of gasoline to produce one pound of feedlot beef.[132] I have watched numerous videos and documentaries and read countless articles and books. It is a business, and the animals are the commodity. No emotions attached. But, at times, as a conscientious consumer, it is hard to stomach, especially knowing the details of confined feedlots:

• Including calves, 35,810,000 heads of cattle are slaughtered every year in the United States.[133]

132 "Food Choices and the Planet," EarthSaveâ, Healthy People Healthy Planet, accessed May 26, 2020.

133 "Annual US Animal Death Stats," 2020 US Animal Kill Clock, Animal-Clock, *Humane Ventures*, accessed June 3, 2020.

- Routine antibiotics, discussed later, are given to prevent disease for a number of reasons, one of which is due to the deplorable living conditions.
- Prepackaged beef is also often irradiated in order to extend the shelf life. Per the FDA, it reduces or eliminates microorganisms and insects, just like pasteurized milk or canned fruits and vegetables.[134]
- Curing beef requires nitrates. Synthetic sodium nitrite is added as a preservative to prevent food spoilage and sickness because it slows bacteria. Sodium nitrite occurs naturally in celery and spinach and is used for curing "uncured" lunchmeat and those "without added nitrites or nitrates." You need to eat *many* servings of beef to reach toxic levels, as regulated by the USDA.[135]
- Growth hormones are often given to stimulate milk production, regulate menstrual cycles, and accentuate sex characteristics in order to accelerate maturity.[136]

These practices are maintained by the major beef companies. Beef is a commodity their customers consume without considering what happens behind the scenes (except for now, during COVID-19, with much more public exposure of the whole process from feedlot or slaughterhouse to package and the terrible working/living environments for the employees). I believe we should be humane in our decision to choose when and how we eat beef, perhaps supporting other means

---

134 "Food Irradiation: What You Need to Know," US Food & Drug Administration, January 4, 2018.

135 "Sodium Nitrite: The Facts," American Meat Institute Fact Sheet, November 2008.

136 "Bovine Somatotropin (bST)," US Food & Drug Administration, April 21, 2020.

of treatment and processing instead of the major US beef corporations: Tyson Foods, Cargill, JBS SA, and National Beef. These four companies own the following brands; the quotes are from each company's website:

- *Tyson Foods*: Tyson, Jimmy Dean, Hillshire Farms, Hillshire Snacking, Ball Park, Raised & Rooted, Aidells
  - "We understand people want to know where their food comes from, which is why we're committed to transparency in all we do. We believe it's our responsibility to steward the land, animals, and resources entrusted to us and ensure we deliver the highest quality food from the farm to your table."[137]

- *Cargill Protein*—North America: Sterling Silver, Angus Pride, Preferred Angus, Rumba, Excel, Our Certified, Corner & Company
  - "Every day, we all wake up wanting to eat better. As people become more prosperous around the world, they are adding animal protein products to their diet as a healthy source of essential nutrients. We work with partners across the food system—from farmers to the world's leading brands—to bring consumers the delicious, convenient, and sustainable protein products they're seeking."[138]

- *National Beef*: Black Canyon Angus, Natural Angus, Corned Beef, Certified Angus, HyPlains Heritage Farms,

---

137 "Getting From Farm to Table," Tyson Foods, accessed May 17, 2020.
138 "Meat & Poultry," Products & Services, Cargill, accessed May 17, 2020.

Certified Hereford Beef, Nature Source, Kansas City Steaks
  – "The foundation of our success is your success. Meaning, integrity goes into every detail. From our commitment to offering high quality beef to being a valued and respected business partner for our suppliers to providing the right solutions to help our customers differentiate in their respective marketplace."[139]

- *JBS USA*: 5 Star, Grass Run Farms, Chef's Exclusive, 1855 Black Angus, Imperial Wagyu Beef, Aspen Ridge, Cedar River Farms, Blue Ribbon, Swift, Showcase, Four Star, Clear River Farms, Certified Angus, La Herencia, thinkpure
  – "Ensuring the well-being of the livestock and poultry under our care is an uncompromising commitment at JBS USA. Our business begins with the well-being of our animals, and we are dedicated to ensuring the humane treatment, handling and slaughter of livestock and poultry."[140]

All four of these companies campaign as conscientious influencers for sustainability, improved animal welfare, decreased environmental impact, and increased transparency. I appreciate the openness. I appreciate the monies devoted to research and development and the focus on efficient practices and employee safety. Luckily, there are resources available for

139 "Quality, Value and Service," Our Mission is Your Success, National Beefâ, accessed May 17, 2020.
140 "Animal Care," 2019 Key Facts and Figures, JBS USA, accessed May 17, 2020.

the conscious consumer in order to know where your beef comes from and how it is raised.

Thankfully, to ease my "omnivore's dilemma," there is the Humane Slaughter Act of 1958, which applied to slaughter-houses/packaging plants supplying the government with meat. It then expanded to all federally inspected meat plants in 1978:[141]

"The Congress finds that the use of humane methods in the slaughter of livestock prevents needless suffering; results in safer and better working conditions for persons engaged in the slaughtering industry; brings about improvement of products and economies in slaughtering operations; and produces other benefits for producers, processors, and consumers which tend to expedite an orderly flow of livestock and live-stock products in interstate and foreign commerce. It is therefore declared to be the policy of the United States that the slaughtering of livestock and the handling of livestock in connection with slaughter shall be carried out only by humane methods."

—HUMANE SLAUGHTER ACT

Per the North American Meat Institute (NAMI), the beef industry has been proactive since the 1990s to increase the quality of animal welfare at its plants. Also, it is public knowledge—posted on the USDA food safety page—when

---

141 "Humane Slaughter Act," United States Code Annotated, Title 7, Agriculture, Chapter 48, Humane Methods of Livestock Slaughter, Animal Legal & Historical Center, Michigan State University, last checked February 2020.

a business is issued a suspension for the inhumane treatment of animals at any point in the production process. One plant received a deferral of enforcement (more like a warning) when a private hauler smacked a cow in the head with a shovel as it exited the trunk down the ramp toward slaughter.[142] Numerous others have had their slaughter lines suspended due to the inability to stun/shoot the animal into unconsciousness in one attempt.

Temple Grandin, PhD, professor of animal science and author specializing in the humane treatment of animals, has worked with the beef industry and has developed systems to ensure the safety of animals and humans involved in processing the cows. She has designed almost half of the chute systems in the US that include a center track restrainer system, focusing on lighting, slow and steady application of the optimal pressure, and nonslip flooring. She continues to share her expert knowledge of animal behavior in order to enhance animal welfare throughout each step of production to ensure the least amount of stress is experienced by the animal. I watched some of her videos with one eye closed, just in case. But she educates with such animation and wisdom that watching an assembly line of cows moving down the shoot to the stunner was manageable. They were calm; her process works.

---

142 "Quarterly Enforcement Report for Quarter 2, Fiscal Year 2020," Regulatory Compliance, United States Department of Agriculture, Food Safety and Inspection Service, accessed June 2, 2020.

She has recently assisted NAMI in establishing the new Animal Handling Guidelines and Audit.[143, 144] Julie Anna Potts, NAMI president and CEO, stated, "The meat and poultry industry is always looking for ways to improve humane animal handling for both the welfare of the animal and the safety of our workforce." These guidelines will assist processing plants with their self-audit to prevent enforcement from the food safety department of the USDA and to drive productivity. As the population increases, the meat industry will want to supply as much product as possible with increased accessibility. Meat/poultry continues to be the largest sector of United States agriculture, which means it also significantly impacts the environment. Therefore, a good number of board members and general counsel are involved in all aspects of promoting animal consumption. They focus on how the industry has changed for the better instead of enlightening the public to all that still needs improvement.

For instance, Potts joined NAMI after having worked at the American Farm Bureau, first as general counsel and then as executive vice president and treasurer. In 2018, she joined NAMI as its president and CEO, bringing an agricultural lobbyist background to the position. There is great crossover between the meat industry and farming, as represented on the board of directors. Potts is two generations removed from the farm but loves to eat, cook, dine, and feel connected to

143 Temple Grandin, "Interpretation of the North American Meat Institute (NAMI) Animal Handling Guidelines for auditing the welfare of cattle, pigs, and sheep at slaughter plants," Grandin, updated January 2020.

144 Temple Grandin, "Recommended Animal Handling Guidelines & Audit Guide: A Systematic Approach to Animal Welfare," Animal Handling, North American Meat Institute, September 2019.

the land. Before she joined NAMI, she spoke at the North Carolina Farm Bureau's annual meeting in 2014.[145] Unbeknownst to me, she stated the mission of my book:

"Consumers want to know more about not just how their food is grown but by whom, and we're well equipped to answer those questions."

—POTTS

She also stated she is committed to "getting it right" for her own children and all children, present and future. This entails supplying abundant nutritious food, good living conditions, educational opportunities, and the best quality of life. She stated American agriculture is the answer.

And, I agree!

---

145 Julie Anna Potts, North Carolina Farm Bureau Federation's Annual Meeting 2014, filmed in Greensboro, NC, December 2014, YouTube video, 8:11-8:21.

"We believe in a future where consumers feel confident in the food they eat and what they feed their families. They trust it. They trust the way it was grown. They have reliable resources about information on how their food and energy are produced and the connection of farming to their own lives. They enjoy tremendous choice and they pay a premium for that choice and farmers benefit from those higher prices. Farmers support the choices of other farmers about what to produce and how to produce it," said Potts.

Potts recently traveled to South Korea and Japan, moving freely throughout South Korea due to the US-Korea free trade agreement. She was impressed by South Korea's detailed presentation of US beef and pork as well as how it was packaged and explained to the consumer. She is hoping for a better US trade agreement with Japan in order to provide more of a favorable outlook to other countries that US beef is a desired commodity.[146]

But we also need to keep it in America.

My friend Michelle's cousin, Jamie, is a cattle rancher in Montana. I asked her what she believes to be the biggest challenges facing farming/ranching today. She stated most ranchers are going broke. "It's so expensive to be in this industry. Especially right now (during the COVID-19 pandemic) cows aren't worth hardly anything. Ranchers invest a lot of money into their cows to be able to ensure they're healthy and top quality. It never was a "get rich" type of job, but right now a lot of people are going broke because we can't even break even since cattle prices are so low. We need Americans to start buying American beef (not imported)."

And think of going directly to the source, if you can. I know most of us do not have room for an entire cow or side of cow, but sharing is caring! Jamie shared her process with me so I could have a better idea about how the money transaction worked: They sell their calves through cattle buyers who are the middlemen; the buyers are paid to find a feedlot who

---

146 "NAMI: Working trade agreements with Japan, South Korea crucial," National Hog Farmer, US Meat Export Federation, April 30, 2019.

will buy the calves; the feedlot then fattens them and tries to sell them to whatever packing plant or rancher/producer they can; the rancher receives nothing once the calf leaves the ranch.

MARKETING

Another industry expert looking to expand the range of beef produced in the United States is Cameron Bruett. He holds many titles at JBS USA (the United States branch of JBS SA, the world's largest beef processor).[147] One of Bruett's titles is chief sustainability officer, which, I imagine, is like riding in the front car of a loop-de-loop roller coaster. In 2015, he stated there is no science-based definition for sustainability, which confuses the beef consumer.[148] Sustainability is defined not as a prescription but an "empowerment tool"; sustainable beef is a socially responsible, environmentally sound, and economically viable product that prioritizes the planet, people, animals, and progress.[149]

"We need to do more with less," Bruett also said. He presented his moral obligation to use as much of the animal as possible and was ashamed of Jamie Oliver for "outing" (or "educating" in other circles) the use of "pink slime," or ground beef trimmings washed with ammonium hydroxide—i.e. lean, finely textured beef—which the FDA claimed

---

147 "Cameron Bruett," JBS USA Leadership, JBS, accessed October 24, 2019.

148 Cameron Bruett, "Defining Sustainability for the Cattle Industry," Texoma Cattlemen's Conference, filmed in Ardmore, OK, March 21, 2015, YouTube video, 4:00.

149 "What is Sustainable Beef?" Global Roundtable for Sustainable Beefâ, accessed October 24, 2019.

to be "generally safe" for use as filler of hamburgers mostly in fast food restaurants.[150, 151] McDonald's restaurants in the United States stopped this practice in 2012. Restaurants in Britain never used pink slime; it is banned in the European Union.[152] McDonald's did not state that Oliver influenced the decision to stop using pink slime, though there was a movement that went viral throughout online sources stating he was singlehandedly responsible.

You can be the judge.

There are those articles, videos, and books I mentioned earlier that compromise the beef industry with images of inhumane treatment of animals and employees, as well as poor processing sequences including sick animals, greenhouse gas emissions statements, and good data for living a vegan lifestyle. "The modern-day consumer is bombarded with so much messaging by biased individuals that it is very difficult to break through all that noise. . . . But the reality for our industry is that demand is growing and our product continues to fly off the shelves. So, we're doing something right," said Bruett."[153]

150 Dr. Elisabeth Hagen, "Setting the Record Straight on Beef," *Health and Safety* (blog), US Department of Agriculture, February 21, 2017.

151 Joel L. Green, "Lean Finely Textured Beef: The 'Pink Slime' Controversy," Congressional Research Service, April 6, 2012.

152 Philip E. Galasso, "Pink slime is banned in Europe, it should be banned in the US," The Citizens' Voice, April 20, 2012.

153 Cameron Bruett, "Defining Sustainability for the Cattle Industry," Texoma Cattlemen's Conference, filmed in Ardmore, OK, March 21, 2015, YouTube video, 4:30.

In an age when most of us, luckily, are free to believe what we want to, there is an overwhelming amount of information to process, including undercover images of confined feedlots and packing plants, beef recalls due to Salmonella or E. coli, and realizations that humanely raised beef is somewhat of an oxymoron. Per Bruett, "Today, you have to collaborate, not with your adversaries (a.k.a. kale and red wine-loving Northeast liberals encouraging people to eat less beef), but with people who you might not necessarily consider an ally."

It is hard to find allies right now, especially when the meat packing industry is wrapped up in the politics of the COVID-19 pandemic, exposing employee safety, and management ills. Food sleuths like Marion Nestle are guiding blog readers through this terrible time when animals are being culled because the food distribution system is broken.[154] Recently, the USDA and other private foundations have bought a portion of the surplus of food to disseminate to who needs it most. Food banks need the donations but cannot receive them because there are not enough packing plants that receive the funding to help the struggling ranchers and farmers manage the surplus.

This is a perfect time to find local sources of beef and learn about the packing industry in your region to see how you can support your local economy. The more you know, the better of a food detective you can be to make the best, tastiest choices.

---

154 Marion Nestle, "Meat: the ongoing saga," *Food Politics* (blog), June 3, 2020.

Another representative of JBS, Kim Stackhouse-Lawson, past director of sustainability research at the National Cattlemen's Beef Association (NCBA) and present director of sustainability at JBS USA (riding the roller coaster next to Bruett), explained a study of one thousand eight hundred people who ate beef at least two times per week.[155, 156, 157] This is how the group rated the order of what is important when buying beef, with quality being at the top:

- Quality, price, value, healthfulness, safety, trusted brand (butcher, farmer, rancher), environmentally friendly, support of causes the consumer believes in.

This is my order of buying beef:

- Quality, environmentally friendly, causes supported, value, safety, healthfulness, trusted brand, price.

If the quality is excellent and you know the impact on the environment, you have had a conversation regarding the practices with the butcher or farmer/rancher. You will then be aware of the effect on your health and that of the animal in order to support your safety and that of the employees producing the beef, at which point you can establish its

---

155 "Kimberly Stackhouse-Lawson," 2018 Award of Distinction Recipients, College of Agricultural and Environmental Sciences, UC Davis, accessed June 3, 2020.

156 "Kimberly Stackhouse-Lawson," Who We Are, Our Sustainability Team, JBS USA, accessed June 3, 2020.

157 Kim Stackhouse-Lawson, Ph.D., "Beef Checkoff Program Sustainability Research," Texoma Cattlemen's Conference, filmed in Ardmore, OK, March 21, 2015, YouTube video, 31:00-33:00.

price-to-value ratio. Price obviously matters for the majority of consumers, and it better be of a good value, especially as it becomes more expensive. More expensive does not always mean better. Therefore, know the source. Hold the package of beef in your hands and close your eyes to see the playback of the story from birth to package. How much can you see? If a lot gets lost, ask questions and do some research.

These are topics discussed by the NCBA surrounding sustainability:[158]

- Responsible, environmentally friendly, humane animal treatment, ethical, conservation, socially conscious, nutrition, family farms, preserves wildlife habitat, local, improves water quality, reduces greenhouse gases, stewardship, improves air quality, treats workers fairly, profitable.

Sustainability is not only about preserving the environment. The average age of a cattle rancher in the United States is fifty-seven years old.[159] Those being trained now need access to capital in order to see a return in their financial investment. People make up the economic and social fabric of this country after all, so the broader educational definition of sustainability is, the more continuous improvement occurs. The needs of the present must be responsibly met while

---

158 Ibid., 34:00-36:00.

159 "Industry Statistics," Beef Industry Overview, National Cattlemen's Beef Association, accessed June 3, 2020.

improving the ability of future generations to responsibly meet their own needs.[160]

The NCBA explains sustainability from their research in a nutshell: meeting the global demand for beef by balancing environmental responsibility, economic opportunity, and social diligence.[161] They are alerting the general public to what has improved: innovations within the food system including crop yields, machinery and irrigation technology, manure management, precision farming, animal performance, biogas capture, closed loop water cooling systems, waste water recycling, and right-size packaging, e.g. a one-pound beef "chub" in a vacuum-sealed package from the packer, which explains the economic side as well. To do less packaging means a win for the company (and the environment!).

At least the NCBA is having the conversation and recognizes our resources are dwindling and there are other strategies that need to be put into place. I am certain these three representatives of the beef/agriculture industry are working with their respective companies to continue to empower ranchers, farmers, and packers to develop improved standards for the health and welfare of their animals in order to sustain the health and wellness of this planet for its citizens, now and in the future.

---

160 Burt Rutherford, "Is sustainability sustainable?" *Beef Editor's Blog* (blog), *Beef Magazine,* March 8, 2017.

161 Burt Rutherford, "Industry Embarks On First Sustainability Study," *Beef Magazine,* February 21, 2013.

THE OTHER CONVERSATIONS

But what happens if that isn't enough for you? It isn't enough for me. Therefore, I rarely buy my meat from a Kroger or Safeway brand supermarket.

An interlude/update: Since initially writing these words, our local supermarket has begun supplying Certified Humane-stamped meat/poultry. I stood there staring at it the last time I perused the meat bins. Now *I* am on the fence. . . .

And resume: I was going to say, "large national retail chain," instead of Kroger or Safeway brand, but Whole Foods Market falls into that category. What's different about Whole Foods, though, versus Safeway or Kroger, is that Whole Foods has created a strict set of guidelines for all beef suppliers to abide by in order for their product to be sold. First of all, beef cattle receive no antibiotics ever, are fed no animal byproducts, are not given added growth hormones and, are raised on pasture for at least two-thirds of their lives. Any item sold in the meat department made with beef, e.g. steak or frozen meatballs, must come from animals raised without antibiotics, synthetic nitrates and nitrates, or added growth hormones, and must be made without hydrogenated fats and artificial colors, flavor, preservatives, and sweeteners. Irradiation is prohibited. It also employs a beef rating system that corresponds to the Global Animal Partnership based upon animal welfare as follows:[162]

---

162 "Meat Department Quality Standards," Whole Foods Market, accessed April 27, 2020.

1. **Animal Welfare Certified**—CertifiedGAP.org (Global Animal Partnership)
    a. Base Level: 100+ standards; no cages, crates, or crowding
2. **Enriched Environment**—enrichments provided to encourage natural behaviors
3. **Outdoor Access**—access to the outdoors with environmental enrichments
4. **Pasture Raised**—no feedlots
5. **Animal Centered**—raised on pasture; no physical alterations
5+. **Entire Life on Farm**—spends entire life on the same farm

Most supermarket chains have established some sort of standards in order to comply with the American Meat Institute Recommended Animal Handling Guidelines and precautions throughout the supply chain in order to ensure their customers are safe to consume what they purchase, guaranteeing the customers will return to buy the same product. Although discouraging any inhumane practices on animals is better than turning a blind eye—which is what some of the chains demonstrate regarding their animal welfare updates—I applaud Whole Foods Market for promoting their Global Animal Partnership. They are advocating for strict guidelines throughout the entire journey, from farm to refrigerator.

———

What I support is the grass-fed movement, GAP animal welfare number four and up. The natural diet of cows is not grain. They are mostly grazers, feasting on grasses and legumes and occasionally eating twigs and leaves. Their digestive system is not equipped to handle grains and, therefore, the millions of cattle raised on feedlots are part of an unnatural order fixed by humans.

Being raised on grains and concentrated mixtures of proteins and high fats, the cows grow faster and fatter, producing more marbling of fat in their meat. Yes, I know this is delicious. . . . but because the digestive tracts are not meant to handle large amounts of grain, antibiotics are required to defend abscesses due to high amounts of built-up acids or bacteria such as E. coli and salmonella.[163] Antibiotics are also used to assist with preventing the spread of disease when cows are raised in very close proximity without any mobility outside of their metal enclosures. As for any mammal, antibiotics are required to keep the host healthy, but they should be used very conservatively.

Therefore, let's talk grass-fed. There are no USDA guidelines on "grass-fed," so it could be grass-fed for one day, forty, or its entire life. There is "grass-finished," which also does not have guidelines. So, when in doubt, find 100 percent grass-fed beef. It will be more expensive because it takes longer for it to get to maximal slaughter weight. It is somewhat controversial to state it is healthier than its grain-fed counterpart.[164] But, if you eat beef, regularly or occasionally, and you want to

163 Ocean Robbins, "The Surprising Truth About Antibiotics, Factory Farms, and Food Recalls," Food Revolution Network, January 18, 2019.

164 Carol Harrison, "Grass-fed or grain-fed beef, what's healthier?" Think Beef, February 28, 2019.

eat the most "natural" form, go with 100 percent grass-fed. It has been found to:[165]

- Be leaner, with less saturated fats;
- Be a better source of omega-3 fatty acids with improved omega-3 to omega-6 fatty acid ratio (essential fatty acids that humans do not synthesize);
- Be free of antibiotics and growth hormones;
- Include improved pre-cursors to Vitamins A and E.

Despite no *significant* health benefits, you're supporting ethics and nature. When buying beef, always ask the butcher, purveyor, or farmer/rancher about the feed. You are entitled to know. If you hear words like "pasture," "compost," "grass," "clover," or "natural environment," you can feel good. If you hear "concentrate," "soy," "corn," "mixed ration," or "intensive production system," say "thank you" and walk away.

Also, something else. My husband and I recently watched a Netflix series sponsored by Bon Appétit magazine presenting professional butchers processing whole sides of livestock.[166] It was mind-blowing to see a) how many pounds of meat are produced from one side of beef, b) how much goes to waste because of how unadventurous the typical beef consumer is, and c) how much the packing industry and supermarkets enable the waste. I highly suggest watching it (you can also watch it on the Bon Appétit YouTube site) to familiarize

---

165 Kris Gunnars, "Grass-Fed vs. Grain-fed Beef—What's the Difference?" Healthline, December 4, 2019.

166 "How To Butcher An Entire Cow—Every Cut Of Meat Explained," *Handcrafted*, Bon Appetit Video, released May 17, 2017.

yourself with the different cuts and how to better use more of the animal.

TAKEAWAYS:

- It takes a tremendous amount of resources to produce one pound of beef.
- The beef industry does its best to be transparent with humane treatment of animals (and humans), but they still support confined feed lots and send US meat overseas.
- The middlemen (the buyers) charge a fee to the ranchers and then negotiate with the next step of the calf's life, making the money—none of which the rancher sees.
- Find your local Whole Foods, or equivalent, for humanely raised beef, minding that grass-fed is the better choice.
- By now, we all know "we are what we eat," so think about it before you buy it. Listen to the story of the journey. Treat yourself humanely. Be an informed food buyer.
- Know how to reduce your footprint by trying something other than filet mignon (again, this is just as important for me as it is for you).

"You create an informed food buyer by giving her some responsibility for her decisions. As a culture, we have governmentally hovered over the food system for so long that the average person doesn't even think about their food. If it's in the grocery store, it's safe. If it has that government inspected label on it, it's okay. . . . but you and I walk to the beat of a different drummer. We can choose wisely."

—JOEL SALATIN

CHAPTER 7:

MEAT ALTERNATIVE —
AN OVERVIEW

Do you see the natural world as needing modification and improvement, or do you see it as something to be observed and interpreted?

—DAN BARBER; MAKER OF YUMMY THINGS, AUTHOR,
REINFORCER OF OBSERVATION AND INTERPRETATION

There was some recent hullabaloo involving an Impossible Whopper. A person who follows a vegan diet decided to order the "burger" but realized it was contaminated by the beef burgers due to it being cooked on the same surface. So, that person is now suing Burger King for false advertising, stating there was no signage alerting consumers to be aware that there is no dedicated cooking area for the Impossible meat. Per the lawsuit, other complaints from a number of consumers state the same information.[167] Burger King now offers this on their website: "For guests looking for a meat-free option, a non-broiler method of preparation is available upon request."[168]

I don't know about you, but I'm somewhat cynical. I imagine a puppeteer, similar to Dr. Claw—the villain in the *Inspector Gadget* cartoon—directing people to situations like this to extort money from corporations by doing really stupid things. (Insert evil laugh here.) I mean, come on. But, I do empathize and do not ever want anyone to be injured, permanently or otherwise. It is just that these situations are preventable, either by the consumer or the person delivering the food and beverage. Hence my cynicism regarding all of this; let's send a vegan to Burger King's drive-through to order an Impossible Whopper that is probably not cooked separately because there is neither the space nor the regard for the particular item since it is fast food—even if it is "cooked to order."

Carl's Jr. sells its Beyond Famous Star with the caveat that it is made for the consumers who do not want to give up beef but can choose to eat less animal protein.[169] I do not know if Carl's Jr. changed its wording on its website once it was made aware of the Burger King lawsuit. They do a much better job of explaining that the Beyond items are not meant to be vegan, nor are they certified vegan. They educate the consumer on how to order if they do prefer to eat vegan.

---

167 Hollie Silverman, "A vegan man claims Burger King cooked Impossible Whopper alongside meat," CNN Business, updated November 19, 2019.

168 Ibid.

169 "Beyond Famous Starâ With Cheese," Menu & Nutrition, Carl's Jr.â, accessed May 26, 2020.

We do seem to be at a crossroads. Reports from climate change scientists suggest that one way we can reduce our carbon footprint is to eat less meat. This is due to the amount of resources used for animal protein production: water, land, machinery, feed. Therefore, you'd think that Impossible and Beyond products would be an excellent recourse, and, sure enough, they certainly seem to be based upon the recent influx of products available for the consumer in the store and restaurant. In fact, Don Thompson, an ex-McDonald's CEO-turned-venture-capitalist has invested in Beyond Meat since 2015 and helped the company go public.[170]

Since going public in May 2019, Beyond Meat's price per share is almost up 700 percent. It opened at $25 and is now trading at $134 per share.[171]

So, to no one's real surprise, a PLT (plant, lettuce, tomato) burger has been in the works at McDonald's test kitchen in Ontario, Canada, since 2019 and is now offered at fifty different McDonald's restaurants throughout Southwestern Ontario.[172] China has requested Beyond products at its Starbucks stores. We shall see if Beyond Meat can, and will, supply the demand of the largest fast food chain in the world.

---

170 Steven R. Strahler, "Don Thompson's fake-meat fortune soars," Consumer products, Crain's Chicago Business, June 7, 2019.

171 Royston Yang, "Why Beyond Meat Soared 29% in May," Nasdaq, June 2, 2020.

172 "P.L.T." Plant. Lettuce. Tomato., McDonalds, accessed June 3, 2020.

TASTE TEST

Neither one of us (my husband and I) had ordered anything Impossible. Until now. A few restaurants in Santa Barbara offer Impossible burgers that look delicious from the descriptions and pictures. Recently we found our way to Burger King; I don't even remember the last time I ate at Burger King. For research purposes, we bought an Impossible Whopper cooked on the grill, an Impossible Whopper non-broiled (microwaved), and a regular Whopper without cheese. Mind you, my husband and I are a sample size of two—not the greatest level of research. We both tasted them blindfolded with the burgers randomized. We both could immediately differentiate the Impossible product and the beef.

The major difference between the broiled and the non-broiled meat alternative was the char from the grill that added additional flavor and texture. The non-broiled Impossible Whopper ended up having very little flavor as compared to the other two sandwiches. But neither of the Impossible Whoppers were bad, per se. In fact, I enjoyed the broiled Impossible Whopper more than the beef. Also, had we not consumed three sandwiches—eaten more slowly than usual—everything would have stayed warmer and, perhaps, juicier. The one that kept its pep was the broiled Impossible Whopper. The other two were sad and hard and required lots of chewing before swallowing to prevent severe choking. I would order the broiled Impossible Whopper again, in an emergency.

We have had our fair share of plant-based burgers, so neither one of us were taken aback by the Impossible Burger's flavor. I introduced my husband nine years ago to MorningStar Farms Grillers Prime Burgers. Prior to that, he had not eaten many veggie burgers, despite being open to eating them. We regularly ate those until I moved away from soy and wheat protein, hence the switch to Beyond and Carla Lee's and Sunshine for legume or nut-based choices. We bought Beyond Burgers regularly when they first hit the shelves. Five dollars and ninety-nine cents per package while being sold in the meat department seemed a little much for bioengineered vegetable protein, but they are flavorful and the juiciest, most accurate color to beef, due to the added beet juice. We usually have one package of them in our freezer. (Since writing, Costco now sells them, so there are three packages in our freezer.) They are also sold at:[173]

- Shop Rite
- Giant Food
- Safeway
- Sprouts Farmers Market
- Target
- Publix
- Ingles
- Walmart
- Kroger

You can now find Impossible Foods (IF) products at the grocery store. When they first launched, it was only restaurants, whereas Beyond was only supermarkets. IF first launched at Gelson's Markets in Southern California. You can now find their products regionally, based on demand:[174]

---

173 "Find Us Near You," Restaurants & Stores, Beyond Meat®, accessed April 27, 2020.

174 "Impossible At Home," Now available in select grocery stores, Impossible™ Foods, accessed April 27, 2020.

- Safeway
- Albertsons
- Pavilions
- Vons
- Gelson's Market
- Jewel-Osco
- Wegmans
- Fairway Market
- Dillons
- Kroger
- H-E-B

I appreciate what IF and Beyond are doing: They are going with the trends and doing a great job of marketing to the general population to a) introduce something as an alternative for omnivores, b) give space to the more environmentally conscious consumer who can only afford fast food, and c) be all-inclusive of diet choice to cater the favorite meal from summertime barbecue to grandma's lasagna to carnitas tacos. It is certainly nice to have choices. And, these alternatives are good choices. IF and Beyond co-won the UN Environment Programme's Champion of the Earth Science and Innovation award in 2018.[175] From the UNEP website:

"Impossible™ Foods and Beyond Meat® are joint winners of the Champions of the Earth Award, in the Science and

---

175 "Champions of the Earth," Annual Report 2018, UN Environment, accessed March 4, 2020.

Innovation category. They produce a sustainable alternative to beef burgers that are more environmentally friendly and rival the taste of meat. These winners believe that there is no pathway to achieve the Paris climate objectives without a massive decrease in the scale of animal agriculture. They are taking steps for the global community to eliminate the need for animals in the food system by shifting to plant-based meat."

CNET blindly taste-tested Impossible and Beyond Meat fixed like traditional cheeseburgers—cheese, lettuce, tomato, sauce—with a sample size of three.[176] Two-thirds of participants preferred the Impossible burger due to its meaty flavor and how it held up as a whole against the rest of the ingredients. But, nobody in my research had told me that their favorite meal was a burger made with either of these products. This discussion is for you to know what exists and what is happening as these two products are making their way into mainstream cuisine.

---

176 Sarah Mitroff, "The ultimate Impossible Burger vs Beyond Meat Burger taste test," Healthy Eating, Health and Wellness, CNET, September 20, 2019.

ENGINEERING

So what is really happening on the journey of an Impossible or Beyond Meat burger? In this case, the process is farm to <u>laboratory</u> to table. Is that okay?

Beyond proudly explains its burger as "the world's first plant-based burger that looks, cooks, and satisfies like beef without GMOs, soy, or gluten. Find it in the meat aisle."[177] As a company, Beyond is "dedicated to improving human health, positively impacting climate change, conserving natural resources, and respecting animal welfare."[178] That sounds great! What I also found interesting is the explanation as to why Beyond discontinued its chicken strips: because the demand was not as great as for the beef and sausage products. Beyond has "a team of chefs and scientists who are working on getting an even better, tastier version of Beyond Chicken Strips back on retail shelves and restaurant menus as soon as possible."[179] Key word: **scientists.**

Beyond compares its work to making pasta. And this could be the comparison at any of the food science labs across the country creating plant-based meat alternatives. The scientists extract from plants all of the core ingredients found in meat—amino acids, lipids, trace minerals, carbohydrates, water—and create a mixture with which to build the same layered texture of meat. They do this through the process of heating, cooling, and compressing the mixture into their different

---

177 "Our Products," Beyond Burger®, Beyond Meat®, accessed April 27, 2020.

178 "Our Mission," Beyond Burger®, Beyond Meat®, accessed April 27, 2020.

179 "Frequently Asked Questions," Beyond Burger®, Beyond Meat®, accessed April 27, 2020.

final products, as if it were linguine, fusilli, or orecchiette. At that point, the chefs take over to see how the products compare to their animal protein counterpart in terms of layered flavor, color, texture, appearance, and stability.

Beyond Meat commissioned the University of Michigan's Center for Sustainable Systems to compare a quarter-pound Beyond Burger with a typical quarter-pound raw beef burger sold at a supermarket.[180] Using the NCBA'S life cycle analysis (LCA) assessment methods from 2017, the researchers determined the life cycle analysis for the Beyond Burger. The meat alternative process used 99 percent less water, produced 90 percent fewer greenhouse gas emissions, used 93 percent less land, and used 46 percent less energy.[181] For a company working to support the environment by conserving natural resources and combat climate change, the data is positive. The research study provided suggestions to lower those numbers even more, such as changing the packaging to include a 100 percent post-consumer recycled polypropylene tray.

The results, no matter what was found, were meant to be shared to maintain the transparency of Beyond Meat's communication with the public and its consumers.

Similarly, IF hired Quantis, the sustainability experts behind many reports on the environmental impact of different

180 Martin C. Heller and Gregory A. Keoleian, "Beyond Meat's Beyond Burger Life Cycle Assessment: A detailed comparison between a plant-based and an animal-based protein source," School for Environment & Sustainability, University of Michigan, *Center for Sustainable Systems*, (September 2018): 1.

181 Ibid.

companies, to provide an updated LCA after IF changed its recipe in 2019.[182] They compared the farm-to-package journey of a one-kilogram Impossible Burger and a one-kilogram frozen ready-to-ship ground beef patty. The meat alternative process used 87 percent less water, used 96 percent less land, produced 89 percent fewer greenhouse gas emissions, and resulted in 92 percent less nutrient polluted run-off.[183]

Beef processing occupies thousands of acres destroying the potential for vital carbon sequestering flora and requires heavy use of freshwater reserves. These reserves are dwindling throughout the United States. Also, beef processing contributes about 3 percent of total US greenhouse gas emissions and has a role in creating previously discussed "dead zones" in coastal ecosystems due to densely polluted nutrient run-off.

THE SCIENCE
Soy: heavy weight, been around for a while, won many fights, owns lots of land, got a bad rap for acting screwy with estrogen, versus Pea: newer to the block, shells out a packed protein punch for its little size, has been growing up recently and getting lots of press for post-exercise recovery. May the best legume win!

What makes the meat alternative taste like beef is the molecule heme. According to IF, leghemoglobin is short for

---

182 Sofia Khan et al., "Environmental Life Cycle Analysis: Impossible Burger 2.0," Executive Summary, Impossible™ Foods, March 2019.

183 Ibid.

legume hemoglobin, the hemoglobin found in soy. Leghemoglobin is a protein found in plants that carries heme, an iron-containing molecule. Heme is essential to plants and animals and is found in every living being. IF discovered heme makes meat taste like meat. IF derives heme from soy plants—which is identical to heme from animals—to give Impossible its uniquely meaty flavor and color.[184]

Initially, IF extracted heme from the root nodules of soy plants. Now, it takes the DNA from the soy plant and combines that with yeast to ferment into heme, "very similar to the way Belgian beer is made."[185] That mixes with soy and potato protein, then some fat and plant-based binders.

The first version of the Impossible Burger (IB 1.0) was not gluten-free due to its second ingredient being textured wheat protein. The Impossible Burger 2.0 (IB 2.0) has been gluten-free since late 2019. Ingredients of the IB 2.0: water, soy protein concentrate, coconut oil, sunflower oil, natural flavors, with 2 percent or less of potato protein, methylcellulose, yeast extract, cultured dextrose, food starch modified, soy leghemoglobin, salt, soy protein isolate, mixed tocopherols (vitamin E), zinc gluconate, thiamine hydrochloride (vitamin B1), sodium ascorbate (vitamin C), niacin, pyridoxine hydrochloride (vitamin B6), riboflavin (vitamin B2), and vitamin B12.[186] For every four-ounce serving, there are:

184 "What is Soy Leghemoglobin, or Heme?" Frequently Asked Questions, Impossible™ Foods, accessed April 27, 2020.

185 "How Do You Make Heme?" Frequently Asked Questions, Impossible™ Foods, accessed April 27, 2020.

186 "What Are The Ingredients?" Frequently Asked Questions, Impossible™ Foods, accessed April 27, 2020.

- 19 g of protein—the same as ground beef
- 0 mg cholesterol
- 14 g total fat (8 g saturated fat)
- 9 g total carbohydrates
- 3 g dietary fiber
- 25 percent of the recommended daily value of iron
- 370 mg sodium
- Less than 1 g of added sugars
- No antibiotics or animal hormones.

Beyond Meat also uses legume protein but focuses on peas, mung, fava beans, and brown rice. Like IF, fat and binders are added to the protein in order to have the same compound as beef. In fact, Beyond Meat has the equivalent amount of or more protein than beef, less fat, and the same complex texture due to the plant-based carbohydrates to create the layered cellular structure.

There is a new "meatier" version of the Beyond Burger that should have arrived by the time this is published. You can search for the red sticker that says, "Now even meatier. Marbled Juiciness. Complete Protein." Ingredients: Water, Pea Protein, Expeller-Pressed Canola Oil, Refined Coconut Oil, Rice Protein, Natural Flavors, Cocoa Butter, Mung Bean Protein, Methylcellulose, Potato Starch, Apple Extract, Pomegranate Extract, Salt, Potassium Chloride, Vinegar, Lemon Juice Concentrate, Sunflower Lecithin, Beet Juice Extract (for color).[187] Despite not focusing on heme as the science driving

---

187 "Our Ingredients," How we make meat from plants, Ingredients, Beyond Meat®, accessed April 27, 2020.

the technology, Beyond Burger has the same amount of iron as Impossible Burger 2.0. Per 4 oz serving:

- 20 g of protein
- 0 mg cholesterol
- 18 g total fat (6 g saturated fat)
- 3 g total carbohydrates
- 2 g dietary fiber
- 25 percent of the recommended daily value of iron
- 390 mg sodium
- 0 g sugars
- No GMO

THE IMPORTANCE

We are talking about examples of lab-grown "meat." This discussion had been eluding me because it slightly tweaks my premise of supporting healthy food grown in healthy soil without much processing so we can be better stewards of our land and resources. As noted above, both meat alternative companies demonstrate remarkable progress toward environmental sustainability, focusing on using less resources as compared to beef production. And I applaud them for that. But what about the genetically modified heme and soy protein? Some people who make the sustainability argument state lab-grown meat is our future, or at least a significant part of it. For instance, Michael Eisen, PhD, professor of molecular and cell biology at UC Berkeley—and consultant for and a shareholder of IF—argues for genetically engineered food. Artificial selection has been done for millennia.

My friend Pam was able to attend college because of GMOs; her father was a farmer in Southern California and bred citrus. She is grateful for science and what farmers, sometimes behaving as geneticists, are capable of. We know more now about the science behind what has and continues to genetically occur as traits appear or disappear. In an article that argues GMOs can save civilizations, Dr. Eisen says,

"Now, if you don't like genetic engineering, you could argue that we don't need plant-based meats. People can (and many do) lead perfectly healthy and happy lives eating other plant-based foods. However, meat—in its many forms—is an integral part of the global diet, and even as people realize the environmental impact of meat, global consumption continues to rise, not fall," which is a point corroborated by the meat industry.[188]

As I researched these companies, I wondered how the pea protein used in Beyond Foods isn't GMO. It turns out it's because the food scientists aren't changing the DNA. The pea protein isolate process starts with grinding yellow peas. Once a fine powder is produced, the starch and fiber are removed, leaving the protein isolate—a concentrated powdered protein. Because it's gritty, it requires the binders and fat to make it more palatable. It is not associated with any allergies, so it is suitable for restricted diets (except for Whole30, which prohibits legumes and, really, all processed foods). So, if you are leading a lifestyle without genetically modified foods, Beyond is your way to go. It is still processed but not GMO.

---

188 Dr. Michael Eisen, Ph.D., "How GMOs can Save Civilization [Impossible Food]," Next Generation Nations™, accessed May 26, 2020.

This book is your self-help guide through food woes. Of course, you'll do what you're going to do. I'm just trying to educate and help you along the journey so you don't have to stare at every product in the grocery store with questions.

TAKEAWAYS:

- Regarding Impossible Foods and Beyond Meat, despite them being in packages and processed, we can say yay for the transparency. Yay for the vegans having something that tastes better than other versions and something made from ethical ingredients.

- Yay for the omnivores offered tasty alternatives to beef in order to make better decisions for ourselves in order to be good stewards, respect the animals, and think about the future of those younger than us.

- I am grateful these options exist and for what their companies represent.

- Impossible Foods and Beyond are leaders and trailblazers, using the research of scientists before them in order to compete with practices that will be difficult to sustain as our population reaches ten billion people across the world.

CHAPTER 8:

EATING SEASONALLY

———

Locally grown, seasonal vegetables help you adapt to your surroundings by subtly connecting you to the rhythm of the seasons.

—KRISTINA TURNER; AUTHOR, WISE
LISTENER AND HEALER WITH FOOD

Pop Quiz!

1. In California, what is NOT at peak season in summer (July–September)?
   a. Cantaloupe
   b. Green beans
   c. Kale
   d. Sweet Corn

2. In the United States, when is winter squash typically harvested?
   a. December
   b. May
   c. August

d. October

3. Tomatoes are typically in season June–October, except in which state?
   a. Alaska
   b. Florida
   c. Tennessee
   d. Vermont

Answers: 1) c; 2) d; 3) b

It is funny to me that this chapter is called "Eating Seasonally." It should just be called "Eating." But, we've ("we" meaning developed countries) gotten so far away from what was, traditionally, called "eating" that "seasonally" has to be specified.

THE ORIGINS

Humans experience many seasons during a lifetime. Humans have also experienced many seasons in terms of evolution of our species. An article published in 2005 in The American Journal of Clinical Nutrition discussed the health implications of the Western diet of the twenty-first century based upon its paleolithic origins.[189] The point: There is evolutionary discordance because of how quickly, in terms of evolutionary history of homo sapiens, we've had to adapt to agriculture and animal "progress." In our adaptation to the changes in the environment, by choice or forced, our genome has become weaker and more prone to disease.

---

189 Loren Cordain et al., "Origins and evolution of the Western diet: health implications for the 21st century," The American Journal of Clinical Nutrition 81, no. 2, (February 2005).

"Similar to all species, contemporary humans are genetically adapted to the environment of their ancestors—that is, to the environment that their ancestors survived in and that consequently conditioned their genetic makeup. There is growing awareness that the profound environmental changes (e.g., in diet and other lifestyle conditions) that began with the introduction of agriculture and animal husbandry . . . occurred too recently on an evolutionary time scale for the human genome to adapt. In conjunction with this discordance between our ancient, genetically determined biology and the nutritional, cultural, and activity patterns in contemporary Western populations, many of the so-called diseases of civilization have emerged."

CORDAIN ET AL. [190]

My point is not to flaunt the paleo diet. I am not a trained nutritionist, but it is within my scope of physical therapy practice to make suggestions. I am demonstrating the historical importance of seasonal eating. There wouldn't have been one single hominid diet but a variety of them based upon geographic region and climate. That hasn't changed as societies have evolved. But, choices would have been "necessarily limited to minimally processed, wild plant and animal foods" instead of Western additions of "dairy products, cereals, refined cereals, refined sugars, refined vegetable oils, fatty meats, salt, or combinations of these foods."[191] As these

---

190 Ibid., 341.

191 Ibid., 342.

additions slowly replaced the hunter-gatherer choices, seven dietary indicators were adversely affected[192]:

1. **Glycemic load**
   a. Potential blood sugar rise due to amount of carbohydrates consumed.
   b. When high, it leads to metabolic syndrome or insulin-related diseases including obesity, cardiovascular disease, type 2 diabetes mellitus, and abnormal cholesterol.
   c. Low in hominin diets

   Moral: Eat more fruit, whole grains, vegetables, and rice; eat less refined flours, refined cereal, and refined sugar.

2. **Fatty acid composition**
   a. Polyunsaturated and monounsaturated fats (good) versus saturated and trans fats (bad).
   b. Saturated and trans fats increase plaques/cholesterol, which increases the possibility of cardiovascular disease.
   c. Major sources of saturated fats in the standard American diet include fatty meats, baked goods, cheese, milk, margarine, and butter.
   d. Only the meat would have been part of hominin diets.

   Moral: Type of fat is more important than quantity of fat; eat less saturated and more poly/monounsaturated fats found in foods like avocado, nuts and seeds, and fish.

---

192 Ibid., 346-350.

3. **Macronutrient composition**
   a. Our meals are based on three: carbohydrate, protein, and fat.
   b. Our caloric intake should be 45–65 percent from carbohydrates, 10-35 percent from proteins and 20–35 percent from fats.[193]
   c. The hunter-gatherer diet consisted of higher amounts of protein (determined by studying their skeletons).[194]
   d. Higher levels of protein intake have been shown to lower cholesterol and help to maintain better blood sugar stability.

Moral: Eat better sources of protein, more often, to maintain stable metabolism; eat non-fatty white fish like cod, haddock, or trout with the occasional salmon, plus nuts, seeds, and sprouts.

4. **Micronutrient density**
   a. Vitamins and minerals
   b. The wild plants of hunter-gatherers had higher levels of micronutrients than those same foods today because some of the nutrients have been lost with the topsoil hodgepodge and heavy machinery.
   c. There has been a displacement of more nutrient-dense foods by less-dense foods, creating significant health problems from vitamin and mineral deficiencies.

---

193 Tracy Rohland, "Fats, Carbs, and Protein: The Balancing Act," Down to Earth Organic & Natural, May 3, 2020.

194 Cordain et al., "Origins," 348.

Moral: Focus on fruits, vegetables, lean meats, nuts, and seeds.

5. **Acid-base balance**
   a. Good old PH balance through the process of digestion, aided by the kidneys; the yield from the foods consumed is either acid or base.
   b. Acid-producing: fish, meat, poultry, eggs, shellfish, cheese, milk, and cereal grains.
   c. Base-producing: fresh fruit, vegetables, tubers, roots, and nuts.
   d. Legumes are neutral.
   e. The typical Western diet yields a net acid load, which means metabolic acidosis or chronic build-up of acid (this taxes the kidneys).
   f. Virtually all preagricultural diets were net base-yielding because of the absence of energy-dense, nutrient-poor foods.

Moral: There is little to no data demonstrating a base yielding diet causes damage; eat more fresh fruit, vegetables, tubers, roots, and nuts.

6. **Sodium-potassium ratio**—my physiology professor in graduate school used his "French Fries Lecture" to demonstrate this, of course with volunteers; it was a riot.
   a. This electrolyte balance interplay assists with daily normal cellular/physiologic function.

b. The rise of the Western diet led to a 400 percent decline in potassium intake while simultaneously initiating a 400 percent increase in sodium intake.[195]

Sodium/Potassium helps with normal heart function and regulates water balance.

c. This imbalance was not part of the hominin diet.

d. The imbalance may contribute to hypertension, stroke, kidney stones, osteoporosis, gastrointestinal tract cancers, asthma, exercise-induced asthma, insomnia, air sickness, high-altitude sickness, and Meniere's Syndrome.[196]

Moral: Eat more fruits, vegetables, fish and whole grains; eat less added salt, vegetable oils, refined sugars, and flours.

7. Fiber content

a. Assists to maintain regularity of gastrointestinal system by enhancing the elimination of waste products.

b. Soluble fibers reduce total and LDL-cholesterol.

c. Our hominin ancestors would not have been lacking in fiber.

Moral: Fiber *is* really good. Eat more of it; it is found primarily in fresh fruit and vegetables including green vegetables, sprouts, and whole grains.

---

195 Ibid., 350.
196 Ibid.

The hunter-gatherers (and less Westernized peoples) followed the seasons and their kill, ate very frugally, used all parts of the produce and animals as they could, and were devoid (as far as we know) of our "diseases of civilization." These diseases are epidemics in contemporary Westernized populations and typically afflict 50–65 percent of the adult population.[197] They can be prevented by really honing into your region and the season, without even looking at labels (imagine that!). So many ingredients to learn about and enjoy.

Another example is from *The Book of Whole Meals*, by Annemarie Colbin.[198] She references a study done in the 1930s by a dentist who studied the teeth of indigenous peoples around the world.[199] The dentist found that tribe members who stayed with the traditional diet of their region presented better teeth quality, better bone formation, and improved strength and endurance. Those who strayed from the diet, who traded with white settlers and ate their sugar, jams, canned vegetables, and white flour, began to display lesser traits in their children, including poorly formed jaws, improper teeth alignment, and a different facial pattern. "In essence, when the quality of the food changed, the people also changed—not only in health but also in appearance."[200] Interestingly, if these children reverted to their traditional diet, *their* children presented classical tribal features, resembling their grandparents.

---

197 Ibid.

198 Annemarie Colbin, *The Book of Whole Meals* (New York: Ballantine Books, 1983).

199 Ibid., 19.

200 Ibid.

When our bodies don't match the environment, they have to adjust. Colbin stated that peeling and eating a banana in Hawaii would feel much better than eating one in Maine when it's snowing outside.[201] And vice versa. Sipping a delicious carrot and bean soup would taste so much better in snowy Maine than sitting on the lanai in Hawaii.

Thanks, Laura, for the background. So now what?

Talking about the hominins and other indigenous tribes hasn't really explained why we should eat seasonally. It only explains what has happened in reaction to the Western diet. I did not write this book to be a dieting book, per se. I wrote it to help you navigate through the food system in order to know how to make the best choices. I see it more as longevity rather than a particular diet. It's a lifestyle. I hope your lifestyle can honor what will prevent the "diseases of civilization."

THE BENEFITS

There are four main reasons why eating seasonally makes sense and why it is part of the story of your favorite meal:

1. It is cheap(er).
- When there is more of something, it tends to be less expensive. Mentally note how much a grapefruit costs in December versus July (and, also, how good they look and smell in December versus July).

---

201 Ibid., 18.

- It costs the central distribution center less money to buy what is abundant, and those savings are passed on to the consumer. Pay attention to the previously discussed Dirty Dozen and Clean Fifteen foods and buy organic if in doubt of processing/fertilizing practices. Even if it's picked early and held in the warehouse, once distributed, it will still be cheaper during its season than out of season.
- Take a walk through your local farmers market and see what comprises the majority of similar products picked at that time of year. Buy that. Plus, because it's fresh and from healthy soil (you hope), it lasts longer, so you can buy less of it.

2. It is healthy(er).
- Up until this point, I haven't really defined the term "healthy." If you have picked up this book, I imagine you already have an idea of what it is. But here is the formal definition, per Merriam-Webster:[202]
  - **Healthy**, adjective
  1a: enjoying good health; free from disease; b: not displaying clinical signs of disease or infection
  2: beneficial to one's physical, mental, or emotional state: conducive to or associated with good health or reduced risk of disease
  3: showing physical, mental, or emotional well-being: evincing good health
    - Doesn't that sound like something you'd like to promote? I'd love to be free from disease and evince good health. All the time.

---

202 *Merriam-Webster*, s.v. "healthy," accessed April 30, 2020.

- Produce picked at peak season has the highest density of nutrients. We want those nutrients, the macro and micro mentioned above, for energy and vitality. Even if not fully ripened on the farm, you will still benefit more from a recently fully-alive head of broccoli in spring through fall than one that's available in late-winter.
- There is also the Eastern philosophy of nutrition and overall wellness; raw fruits and vegetables make sense for the summertime to assist in cooling us down. But come winter, that same focus will make us feel cold and damp. If the salads are replaced by more hardy foods like root vegetables, cabbages, squashes, and dried fruit, resistance to cold weather increases.[203, 204] We create a pattern to connect with our environment, just like the protagonists of the movie *Avatar*.[205]

"When we consume food that grows in a particular climate, we will feel more 'at home' in that environment, for by consuming part of that environment we have made it part of ourselves."

—ANNEMARIE COLBIN

203 Annemarie Colbin, *Whole Meals*, 19.

204 Kristina Turner, *The Self-Healing Cookbook: Whole Foods to Balance Body, Mind & Moods* (Vashon Island: Earthtone Press, 2002), 63.

205 *Avatar*, written and directed by James Cameron, (2009; Los Angeles, CA: Twentieth Century Fox), film.

3. You manifest a smaller carbon footprint.
- This can be a sticky topic. Let's discuss this for a moment. In developed countries, as mentioned earlier, we are slammed by tens of thousands of products the moment we walk into a supermarket or big box store. We can get anything and everything we want twelve months a year. Way to go for technology, engineering, and smart people. We didn't know we needed any of that, but thank you!

Stop. Where does it all come from?

- Oregon and Maine: Who knew you needed fresh blueberries in February from Peru? New Mexico and Rhode Island: How good do sweet potatoes from New Zealand sound in April? West Virginia: What about lemons in . . . wait . . . lemons don't grow in West Virginia. Oh no! Does that mean that West Virginians (and most residents of the United States for the same reason) can't enjoy lemonade, lemon merengue pie, or chicken piccata? In 1920, probably. In 2020, no way. Keep in mind, though, where the lemons are coming from. The closest state to West Virginia that produces abundant citrus is Florida. Since you know that citrus season is winter, try to find lemons not from Argentina in winter. California would be okay because, really, lemons are grown year-round and despite the lemons still being treated with a fungicide to prolong shelf life and keep them from dying in refrigeration, travel time and distance is almost half of what it is from South America.[206] And, that produce will have been given

---

206 "Seasonal Food Guide," Find what's in season near you, Seasonal Food Guideâ, accessed April 27, 2020.

some sort of stabilizer to prevent it from dying—a wax and/or a gas. Yuck.

I am just as guilty as the rest of you who want lemons in water, with fish, on chicken, in a dessert year-round. We have that ability. This book is about you being aware and about empowering your voice of reason before you put something into your basket.

- In general, your carbon footprint will be smaller because your food isn't traveling across the globe. It's a win for the environment, and you're doing your part to allow the earth to feed the ten billion people expected to inhabit the earth by 2050. Most likely, your food is sourced locally/regionally because you are eating what is at peak harvest for that time of year, where you are. Therefore, it doesn't travel very far, thus saving on carbon emissions, making you feel good for keeping it local and supporting your local producers.
- Bonus: You're also putting the money back into your local economy. And you'll be able to ask and see what sort of growing practices are used. Who knows what sort of pesticides were used on the tomatoes imported from Mexico? Also, there is a tremendous amount of produce that rots in transit. You don't want to promote waste.

4. It tastes better
- This involves the peak amount of nutrients mentioned above in number two. And the feeling you get when you bite into an ear of fresh sweet corn in the summer from the local farm stand or into an apple right off the tree at the u-pick farm in the fall.

- Typically, the longer something sits, the less flavor it has. And if it has sat in a truck or on a plane in a crate, I guarantee you it won't taste as good as it would have off the vine or out of the ground. And it was probably picked early to ripen in a crate, out of the sun.

The most beneficial aspect is that you get to experience such a wide variety of foods. I realize the variety is determined by where you live. Each state/region has its own climate and growing patterns. If you grew up where you live, you'll know what to look for in your markets and what tastes best at its peak. Search for signs of "'local" in your supermarket or grocery store. Shop as much as you can at the farmers market or farm stand. If there is something you're not familiar with, ask the grocer or the seller. You'll learn the history and, hopefully, tricks on how to eat the produce to make it taste its best.

BUT, IS IT PRACTICAL?
Yes. Okay, next chapter! Just kidding.

This brings up my last point, which is an addition from my husband, Davis, and one that is valid. I mentioned waste earlier. Think about the fruit and vegetables that have traveled across the country or world to get to your local store. If it's there, why not buy it? If it isn't bought, it will be wasted, go to the landfill, and produce methane, which destroys the ozone layer and is contributing to global warming. So, therefore, we should buy it. It's fresh, or once was. It might even be organic.

Talk about guilt.

The point is to promote a lifestyle that decreases the demand for Peruvian blueberries in January. If more people focus on seasonal eating and supporting local growers, those blueberries can stay in Peru and that land can be used for food for Peruvians and other South Americans.

TAKEAWAYS:

- You know to look for what's abundant and affordable. If you see the price of an item drop $1–2 per pound, it's most likely harvest time, or was recently harvested.
- Most of the produce shipped across the country to the chain supermarkets come from California, Texas, Arizona, Oregon, Washington, and Florida. Additionally, much of it comes from Mexico and South America when it isn't in season or if your state does not grow particular items at all.
- If you must buy something from the produce section in a plastic container, look for the "product of" fine print. You make the choice if it's from a land far, far away.
- Listen to your hominin ancestors who were disease-free and take a step back to observe what we have done to our "evolved" selves, with our changed food patterns and lifestyle diseases. It isn't complicated.

CHAPTER 9:

BEING THE DETECTIVES

———

We are up against weapons of mass expansion and we are losing the battle.

—MARK HYMAN, MD; GURU OF NUTRIGENOMICS,
AUTHOR, ULTIMATE ADVOCATE, WARRIOR

Elvis Costello sings about watching the detectives.[207] I want you to *be* the detectives. Channel your inner Benson, Drew, Holmes, Poirot, or Columbo. With how overwhelming our food system has become, the skillsets of these characters could be something important to glean.

My own version to the tune of *Watching the Detectives*:

Nice foods, not one with a defect

Cellophane shrink-wrapped, so correct

———

207 *Watching the Detectives*, written and performed by Elvis Costello, Stiff Records (UK), released October 1977.

So tempting like hot dogs, pizza, the deli

Tell me, where can I find the peanut butter and jelly?

I know the majority of you shop at the supermarket. Let's face it. It's easy. It's convenient. It's accessible and cheaper. So, here is where it gets fun. Here is where I want you to have a homing device. You walk in and see the approximately thirty-five thousand items and know you have to make some choices. For instance, for my favorite meal, I need to buy beef, potatoes, cream, butter, rosemary, lemons, and broccoli. I already have salt and pepper at home. At our local supermarket, I can get organic potatoes, cream, butter, lemons and broccoli—all located on the right-hand side of the store, so I can bee-line it for the produce and then head toward the back to the cream and butter. And because I live in California, I can get these items year-round. I bet you can too, at your equivalent. When available, I buy them at the farm stand or farmers market instead, which would then be spring or fall for the broccoli, winter-ish for the lemons, and spring or fall for the potatoes. I'll buy the rosemary from the herb section at the store or from an herb farmer.

Despite stating earlier I'm "on the fence," I will rarely buy the beef at the larger chain supermarket. I will continue to go to a specialty market or farmers market for grass-fed, pasture-raised beef.

The only possibly packaged item is the rosemary, which includes only the herb, but a bunch of sprigs tied together with a twisty tie would be better.

Your meal might require more items to buy, or maybe you are reworking yours in your head at this point to make it more environmentally or ethically friendly. This is where you break out your homing device for the labels—the labels!—and blast through them. They aren't meant to be confusing, but they are. I already discussed some commonly found ingredients in The Storytellers chapter when using Michael Pollan's research to prove my point about making better choices for more whole foods and less human-made fillers (because many people are already getting filled up by too much!).

What I'd like to do is emulate (and be her when I grow up) food politician Marion Nestle, PhD, Paulette Goddard professor emerita of nutrition, food studies, and public health at New York University. She is not related to the Nestle who the majority of us know. There is no "ee" sound at the end of her name; it's pronounced like the verb, to nestle. In *What to Eat*, she painstakingly figured out the background of the nutrition labels and why they are laid out as they are.[208]

In 1990, Congress passed the Nutrition Labeling and Education Act (NLEA).[209] The statute directed the FDA to require nutrition labeling of most foods as regulated by the FDA. All nutrient content and other health claims, e.g. "high fiber" or "low fat," were consistent with preexisting dietary regulations of the FDA.

---

208 Marion Nestle, PhD, *What To Eat* (New York: North Point Press, 2006), 6.

209 Richard Williams, Michael L. Marlow, Edward Archer, "Retrospective Analysis of the Regulations Implementing the Nutrition Labeling and Education Act of 1990," Regulation, Mercatus Center, George Mason University, April 12, 2016.

There is a lot of information packed into that fine print. You—the consumer—are supposed to understand the label and to know how the information fits into your total diet for the day. This makes sense if you a) study nutrition or have a basic idea of the macronutrients, b) know how many calories you should be consuming in order to maintain your health, c) can do math easily or have a calculator handy, and d) can read English. Good grief.

NUTRITION BASICS AND LABELS

A quick layout of the nutrient information for daily suggestions:

DRVs — Food Components					
Food Component	Unit of measure	Adults and Children ≥ 4 years	Infants through 12 months	Children 1 through 3 years	Pregnant women and lactating women
Fat	Grams (g)	[1]78	30	[2]39	[1]78
Saturated fat	Grams (g)	[1]20	N/A	[2]10	[1]20
Cholesterol	Milligrams (mg)	300	N/A	300	300
Total carbohydrates	Grams (g)	[1]275	95	[2]150	[1]275
Sodium	Milligrams (mg)	2,300	N/A	1,500	2,300
Dietary Fiber	Grams (g)	[1]28	N/A	[2]14	[1]28
Protein	Grams (g)	[1]50	N/A	[2]13	N/A
Added sugars	Grams (g)	[1]50	N/A	[2]25	[1]50

[1] Based on the reference caloric intake of 2,000 calories for adults and children aged 4 years and older, and for pregnant women and lactating women.

[2] Based on the reference caloric intake of 1,000 calories for children 1 through 3 years of age.

DRV, or daily reference value, is the recommended maximal daily intake of each food component; you can gauge the health of one serving size by using this reference. For instance, if one serving size of something has 20 grams of saturated fat, you'll eat your recommended daily allowance of saturated fat in that single serving. Basically, if you eat the cookie, you cannot have the steak and mashed potatoes later for dinner.

When Congress passed the original NLEA, the FDA used serving sizes based on studies of food consumption in 1977–78 and 1987–88. How many times have you reluctantly closed the bag after eating four potato chips saying, "That's it?"

There's a point to that, people! Think about the consequences.

But per the FDA, "The serving sizes listed on the Nutrition Facts label are not recommended serving sizes. By law, serving sizes must be based on how much food people *typically* consume, and not on what they *should* eat."[210]

So, thirty years later there has been a change to the labeling system to reflect how much people are typically consuming in one sitting—definitely not only one-third of a muffin or one-fourth of a pint of ice cream. For instance, twelve-ounce and twenty-ounce sodas are both now one serving. The previous serving size of half a cup of ice cream has increased to two-thirds of a cup.

- Huh? I explained that to my husband and he says that makes no sense. How can twelve ounces *and* twenty ounces be one serving, and how can one serving of ice cream all of a sudden change? Follow me with this parallel. It also reflects what has happened with clothing in the same time frame. Davis is six feet tall and has always weighed around 150 pounds. Thirty years ago, he wore a

---

210 "Food Serving Sizes Get a Reality Check," Food & Beverages, US Food & Drug Administration, July 16, 2016.

large t-shirt. Now, he wears a small and sometimes can fit into an extra small.

- Great! I can now fit into a small shirt. Give me that almost-cup of ice cream!
- Oompa Loompa, doompadee do, I've got another puzzle for you![211]

- It actually means that clothing has had to shift to manage a larger-sized population. A small t-shirt in 2020 is actually a large from 1988.[212] Both the food and clothing industries are misleading the public, doing nothing to assist the obesity epidemic.
- Granted, as the serving size increased, the nutrition facts have also demonstrated the increase.

The changes to the serving size were supposed to simplify understanding, allowing people to make the choice (or not) to eat the entire serving after seeing what they would consume in terms of calories, fat, fiber, sugar, carbohydrates, vitamins/minerals, and their percentages of the daily caloric intake (generally based on 2,000 calories per day). Follow the DRV chart for reference. "We hope that updating the label in these ways makes it easier for people to be more realistic about the number of calories and nutrients they're actually consuming and to make healthier choices when choosing foods for themselves and their families," says Douglas

---

211 *Willy Wonka & the Chocolate Factory,* directed by Mel Stuart, written by Roald Dahl, lyrics and music by Leslie Bricusse and Anthony Newley (1971; Beverly Hills, CA), film.

212 Laura Stampler, "The Bizarre History of Women's Clothing Sizes," *Time,* October 23, 2014.

Balentine, PhD, the director of the FDA's Office of Nutrition and Food Labeling.[213]

The point: Read the ingredients and look at the numbers. How many servings per package is stated at the top. Pay attention. The percentage of recommended daily intake is listed with each component per one serving size so you can determine how much of your daily recommended value you will consume with each serving. If there are a lot of ingredients, especially ones that are hard to pronounce, ask yourself how much you really need it. Look at the amount of carbs, fat, protein, and other components to gauge the health of the product.

SPONSORED HEALTH CLAIMS

The other aspect of labels are the health claims. Traditionally, both the American Heart Association (AHA) and American Diabetes Association (ADA) have sponsored many food products as heart healthy or as part of a diet to reduce the risk of diabetes.[214, 215] Keep in mind that, despite strict requirements per the two organizations to be a part of the sponsorship programs, there are loopholes and non-transparencies; they both receive funding from pharmaceutical companies. But they both do an excellent job of demonstrating ways to

213 "Food Serving Sizes Get a Reality Check," Food & Beverages, US Food & Drug Administration, July 16, 2016.

214 "Heart-Check in the Grocery Store," Company Collaboration, American Heart Association, accessed May 3, 2020.

215 "What Can I Eat?" Nutrition Overview, American Diabetes Association, July 18, 2019.

promote wellness through the education presented on their websites.

Here are the requirements for a food product to be included in the AHA Heart-Check Food Certification Program:[216]

- Standard Certification (FDA-regulated products)
  - Total fat: less than 6.5 g.
  - Saturated fat: 1 g or less and 15 percent or less calories from saturated fat.
  - Trans fat: Less than 0.5 g.
  - Cholesterol: 20 mg or less.
  - Sodium: Depends on the particular food category; up to 140–480 mg per label serving.
  - Beneficial nutrients (naturally occurring): 10 percent or more of the daily value of 1 of 6 of the nutrients vitamin A, vitamin C, iron, calcium, protein, or dietary fiber.

- There are additional requirements that involve sugar and fiber:
  - Canned fruits/vegetables: No "heavy syrup" (including potatoes and sweet potatoes).
  - Frozen fruit: 100 percent fruit (no added sugar).
  - Fruit/vegetable juice: 100 percent juice (or 100 percent juice plus water) with no added sugars/sweeteners (excludes non-nutritive sweeteners)
    - 120 calories or less per 8 fluid ounces

---

216 "How a Food Becomes Heart-Check Certified," Company Collaboration, American Heart Association, accessed May 3, 2020.

- 10 percent daily value or greater for three nutrients for which a daily value exists. At least one of these beneficial nutrients must satisfy the beneficial nutrient requirement listed above.
  - Grain-based products: All grain-based products must be a good source of dietary fiber (10 percent or more DRV) and contain 7 g or less total sugars per serving if the product is a good source of dietary fiber (10–19 percent DRV) or 9 g or less total sugars per serving if the product is an excellent source of dietary fiber (20 percent or more DRV)
    - Sugars from pieces of fruit do not count toward the sugars allowance, but amount(s) and source(s) must be disclosed.
  - Grain-based snack bars: must be a good source of dietary fiber (10 percent or more DRV) and contain 8 g or less of added sugar per serving
  - Milk and milk alternatives: 130 calories or less per 8 fluid ounces
  - Snacks: 5 grams or less of added sugar per serving. Naturally occurring sugars do not count toward this limit.
    - Grain-based snacks: must be a good source of dietary fiber (at least 10 percent DRV)
  - Yogurt: 20 g or less total sugar per standard 6 oz serving

Foods not considered for AHA Heart-Check program:

- Alcoholic beverages
- Candy and confections
- Desserts, including:

- Brownies, cakes (all), candied fruit, cookies, custard and pudding, gelatin, doughnuts, Danishes, sweet rolls, toaster pastries, eclairs and cream puffs, grain-based dessert bars (i.e. fig bars), ice cream, ice milk, frozen yogurt and sherbet, frozen flavored ice and pops, frozen fruit juice bars, gelato, pie filling, pies, cobblers, fruit crisps, turnovers, and other pastries
- Dietary supplements
- Diet-branded and weight-loss products
- Foods containing partially hydrogenated oil (trans fat)
- Medical foods
- Meal replacements

The ADA does not devote space on its website for the requirements for product sponsorship.

I do love what the ADA states on its website right now as we are all managing grocery shopping while trying to maintain health during the COVID-19 pandemic: "Now is a great time to be inspired to cook at home, sit down to family meals, slow down, enjoy the food we eat, and be a little more mindful. Staying at home can be stressful for sure, but there are silver linings!" I just said something similar in an Instagram video recently. The silver linings: cooking more, being with family, learning new ingredients, knowing what's in your food! The ADA has partnered with Blue Apron, the home food delivery service that provides portion control. It also offers these hints for decoding nutrition facts labels on its website under the Nutrition section, as follows:[217]

---

217 "Navigating Nutrient Claims," Understanding Food Labels, American Diabetes Association, accessed May 3, 2020.

- **Calories**
  - Calories free: less than 5 calories per serving
  - Low calorie: 40 calories or less per serving

- **Fat**
  - Fat free: less than 0.5 g of fat
  - Saturated fat free: less than 0.5 g saturated fat
  - Trans fat free: less than 0.5 g trans fat
  - Low fat: 3 g or less of total fat
  - Low saturated fat: 1 g or less saturated fat
  - Reduced fat or less fat: at least 25 percent less fat than the regular version

- **Sodium**
  - Sodium free or salt free: less than 5 mg of sodium per serving
  - Very low sodium: 35 mg of sodium or less
  - Low sodium: 140 mg of sodium or less
  - Reduced sodium or less sodium: at least 25 percent less sodium than the regular version

- **Cholesterol**
  - Cholesterol free: less than 2 mg per serving
  - Low cholesterol: 20 mg or less
  - Reduced cholesterol or less cholesterol: at least 25 percent less cholesterol than the regular version

- **Sugar**
  - Sugar free: less than 0.5 g of sugar per serving
  - Reduced sugar: at least 25 percent less sugar per serving than the regular version

- No sugar added or without added sugars: no sugar or sugar-containing ingredient is added during processing

- **Fiber**
    - High fiber: 5 g or more of fiber per serving
    - Good source of fiber: 2.5–4.9 g fiber per serving

The ADA promotes a balanced diet of fruits and vegetables, lean meats and plant-based sources of protein, and less added sugar and less processed foods. It suggests people to look for lower-cost options such as fruit and vegetables in season or frozen/canned fish. Foods easier on the budget year-round are beans and whole grains that you cook from scratch. Yes!

There are just two examples of companies supporting claims that you might notice on products. Both the AHA and ADA are non-profit organizations. The ADA is financed primarily by drug companies. The majority of the AHA is funded by private non-corporate donations, but it does receive a portion from pharmaceuticals. Both the AHA and ADA provide a significant amount of information on maintaining a healthy and well-balanced life, not only for patients with cardiovascular dysfunction or diabetes, but for the general populace as well.

Associated with these health claims are food studies, sometimes used as backup for product sponsorship. Per the labeling act, these health claims:

- Must contain the elements of a substance and a disease or health-related condition;

- Are limited to claims about disease risk reduction;
- Cannot be claims about the diagnosis, cure, mitigation, or treatment of disease;
- Are required to be reviewed and evaluated by FDA prior to use.
  - "To be approved by the FDA as an authorized health claim, there must be significant scientific agreement (SSA) among qualified experts that the claim is supported by the totality of publicly available scientific evidence for a substance/disease relationship. The SSA standard is intended to be a strong standard that provides a high level of confidence in the validity of the substance/disease relationship."[218]

This is what Nestle has to say about that in her new book, *Unsavory Truth*:[219]

"Whenever I see a study suggesting that a single food (such as pork, oats, or pears), eating pattern (having breakfast), or product (beef, diet sodas, or chocolate) improves health, I look to see who paid for it. This is possible because most professional journals now require scientific articles to include special sections where authors must disclose who paid for their study and whatever financial arrangements they might have with the funder or a similar company. . . . It is much easier to find industry-funded studies with results favorable to the sponsor's interests than those with unfavorable results."

218 "Questions and Answers on Health Claims in Food Labeling," Food Labeling & Nutrition, US Food & Drug Administration, December 13, 2017.

219 Marion Nestle, *Unsavory Truth* (New York: Basic Books, 2018), 35.

OTHER LABELS

If you must buy something that is in a package, don't let the marketing get you. "Healthy!" "Whole grain!" "Made with real fruit!" "The same amount of calcium as eight ounces of milk!" "All-natural!"

There is one group that I'd like to finish up with, one that is the most difficult for me: eggs. Well, I guess, hens. I want to flush out the labels for eggs, but I won't be getting into poultry politics.

This list is compiled from the websites of Humane Farm Animal Care (Certified Humane) and the Humane Society.[220, 221] These are the claims on egg cartons. Watch out for the sneaky ones—they'll get you! (Spoiler alert: Chickens have beaks. Bad things have to happen in order for thousands of them to manage very tight spaces and stay alive.)

- "Conventional"
  - Grain-fed, given supplements of vitamins and minerals.
  - Beak cutting and forced molting by starvation occur.
  - Caged.
  - White eggs have the same nutritional value as brown; brown hens are larger and require more feed, hence the expense put forth to the consumer.

---

220 "How to decode egg labels," Certified Humane Raised & Handled, accessed May 3, 2020.

221 "How to decipher egg carton labels," A guide to egg labels, The Humane Society of the United States, accessed May 3, 2020.

- "Omega-3," an essential fatty acid our body cannot produce, therefore we need it from food and some egg producers have started to fortify feed with sources of omega-3.
  - Raised conventionally.
  - It is hard to regulate how much omega-3 is absorbed into the egg matter.
  - Feed includes flax seed and is sometimes fortified with fish oil (which humans can do, too, for their diet).
  - Contains more omega-3 than conventional or organically fed chickens.
    - Omega-3 does not need to be consumed from flax treated eggs; it is also found in chia seeds, hemp seeds, walnuts, and soy/beans.

- "Natural"
  - Pertains only to the food: minimally processed without artificial ingredients.
  - Beak cutting and forced molting by starvation occur.

- "No Added Hormones or Antibiotics"
  - Just a ploy to have the consumer think that other farmers are using them! Confusing.
  - Federal regulations have banned the use of growth hormones since the 1950s.[222]
  - Beak cutting and forced molting occur.

- "Non-GMO"
  - Just like "organic"; a GMO-free diet for the chickens.

---

222 Alice Mitchell, "Chicken Producers Don't Use Growth Hormones—Here are the Reasons Why," Poultry Health, The Poultry Site, April 12, 2016.

- Beak cutting and forced molting occur.

- "Vegetarian-Fed"
    - Chickens are not vegetarians, but in this case, they are not fed ground-up chicken, nor other animal byproducts.
    - Beak cutting and forced molting occur.

- "Organic"—regulated by the USDA
    - It only pertains to the food the chickens eat.
    - Feed is without synthetic fertilizers, sludge, irradiation, or GMOs.
    - Beak cutting and forced molting occur.

- "Cage-Free"—regulated by the USDA
    - Hens can move freely throughout their space and have unlimited access to food and water while still producing eggs.
    - There is no regulated amount of space given, though, and no outside access.
    - Beak cutting and forced molting occur.

- "Free-Range"—regulated by the USDA
    - Chickens have continuous access to the outdoors, which might be fenced or netted.
    - There is no regulated meaning of "outside access."
    - Beak cutting and forced molting occur.

- "Pasture-Raised"
    - Federally unregulated; anyone can claim the label.
    - Beak cutting and forced molting still occur, unless the hens are raised humanely (see below).

- "Humane"
  - Federally unregulated; anyone can claim it.

- "United Egg Producers Certified"—the majority of egg producers are included in this program
  - Promotes inhumane practices, according to The Humane Society.
  - Beak cutting, but no forced molting, occurs.
    - Caged: each bird has 0.46 square feet (smaller than a sheet of paper).
      - Battery-operated cages.
      - No perching, nesting, foraging, or spreading their wings.
    - Cage-free: uncaged, but inside at all times, with 1 square feet of indoor space per bird.
      - Some perching and nesting requirements permitted.

- "American Humane Certified"
  - Beak cutting, but no forced molting, occurs.
    - Cage-free: uncaged, but may be kept inside at all times with 1.23 square feet per hen with access to perch and nest.
    - Free-Range: uncaged, 21.8 square feet per bird of outdoor access.
    - Pasture-raised: 108 square feet per bird, without specified amount of time outdoors on living vegetation.
    - Must be able to perch, nest, and dust bathe.

- "Food Alliance Certified"
  - Beak cutting, but no forced molting, occurs.

- No animal byproducts in the feed.
  - Cage-free: 1.23 square feet of inside space per bird.
  - Access to outdoor area or daylight for eight hours per day with living vegetation.
  - Must be able to perch, nest, and dust bathe.

- "Certified Humane"—determined by Humane Farm Animal Care
  - The Certified Humane label assures consumers that farmers are adhering to a precise set of Animal Care standards.
  - Beak cutting, but no forced molting, occurs.
  - No cage systems are allowed; hens are allowed to dust bathe and forage.
  - There is a gradual decrease from light to dark to maintain normalcy and prepare for dark.
  - 1–1.5 square feet of space per bird.
    - Free-range: hens have daily access to uncovered outdoor area, six hours per day, allowed 2 square feet per bird.
    - Cage-free: uncaged but may be kept inside at all times; must be able to perch, nest, and dust bathe.
    - Seasonally pasture-raised: outside on pasture, weather permitting.
    - Pasture-raised: 2.5 acres per one thousand birds or 108 square feet per bird, outside during the day in living pasture for at least six hours, kept indoors at night.

- "Animal Welfare Approved"—the highest standards, per the Humane Society
  - No beak cutting or forced molting.

- No animal byproducts in the feed.
- Flocks are less than five hundred birds.
- 1.8 square feet of indoor space per bird.
- Continuous access to the outside covered by living vegetation, 4 square feet of space per bird.
- Must be able to perch, nest and dust bathe.

Just like cows, chickens are a commodity and treated almost like machines. I mean, breakfast is served all day at McDonalds, so they have to be pumping out those eggs for the Egg McMuffins, right?! I love eggs, but chickens also deserve to be treated well and thanked for their service. By giving them space and as natural of a habitat as possible, your eggs can be that much more sublime. You should see the ones we got from the farm stand recently. Each shell is a different hue of gray or tan and strong; the yolk is huge and silky and beautifully golden yellow. And, they last a long time in the refrigerator.

SOLVING THE CASE

This has been a lot of information. I hope you don't feel too scrambled or fried! (I couldn't resist). What does Olivia Benson do when she feels stuck?[223] She looks at the facts. She asks herself, "How does this connect to what I'm trying to achieve with this case?" I want you to ask yourself, "How does this box of AHA supported cereal or these Open Nature chicken thighs connect to what I'm trying to achieve with my favorite meal in order for it to be the tastiest and most healthful?"

---

223 "Captain Olivia Benson," portrayed by Mariska Hargitay, Law & Order Special Victims Unit, created by Dick Wolf (New York, NY: NBC Studios, 1999-2020), television series.

TAKEAWAYS:

- Have an idea of the ratio of carbohydrates to fat to protein your body responds well to and follow that routine when looking at DRV facts on labels.

- Remember that serving sizes have recently increased due to how much more Americans are eating now than in the 1970s and '80s. You do not *have* to eat the two-thirds cup of ice cream if the half-cup was satisfying.

- Despite non-profit organizations promoting health and wellness with different programs, you do not have to buy a product just because they have sponsored it as there is usually money involved. You know what to look for on the labels to gauge if those claims are true. Don't let the marketing ploys suck you in.

- Try to buy Animal Welfare Approved or Certified Humane raised eggs at the supermarket. It's worth the extra bucks. Or ask at the farmers market how the hens are treated.

- You are in control. Get out your homing device, sweep across the store, and figure out the best choices. It is exciting, and you might be surprised by what you find!

CHAPTER 10:

CHOICES

———

Because so often when we say we're unqualified for something, what we're really saying is that we're too scared to try it, not that we can't do it.

—JEN SINCERO; AUTHOR, THE BUTT KICKER, DEFENDER OF AN AWESOME LIFE

What if you were told to listen to an album claimed to be "the greatest of all time" and, upon finishing, didn't like it? You listen again and still don't like it. Is it you? Is it okay to not agree?

So much of what we have in our lives nowadays is because of reviews. Other people's opinions. Why do they get to have a piece of our story? Because that story is now about the destination, not about the journey. Yes, I'm giving you opinions on what I promote to be healthy, but I am also referencing the scientific evidence regarding soil health, decreased use of fertilizers and pesticides, and improved ethical treatment of animals to support my claims. I am not a farmer. I am not a nutritionist. This evidence is from research both from journalists and anecdotally from the field. But, despite this, there are still people who refute the science (since when is climate change a "belief" like Santa Claus or the Easter Bunny?) and those whose opinions do not jive with shopping at an organic farm stand because of politics. That is still part of their journey. As long as they do not harm me, I will give them the grace to agree to disagree.

BEHIND THE SCENES
My friend Mike is a chef in New York City. He's been around the world, so I love learning about food from him. But he's also that person who looks straight through you and calls, "Bullshit." He wouldn't be ashamed for me to say he and bullshit don't mix. So, if you try to deal it, he'll push it straight back to you. This works in some kitchens but not in others, so when he was given the opportunity to be executive chef, he grabbed it. He would finally be able to put together his team and, hopefully, deal with less BS.

Unfortunately, there were other people in the pool: investors, management, and owners, who all liked to throw in their opinions despite Mike creating the menus and, ultimately, being responsible for the restaurant's success. At his last venture, he was told, "You know, we really should have a burger on the menu." That was like him being told to listen to "the greatest album of all time" and not liking it. He attempted to gracefully say no, but because he wasn't really in charge, he acquiesced. He put a burger on the menu in between the delicious octopus appetizer and the perfect duck confit. This wasn't what caused the restaurant to close, of course. There were many variables including the investors, the management, and the owners. Plus, there was the (social) media.

In 2014, Mike was interviewed by *The Village Voice*, a newspaper for everything arts, food, and culture.[224] He was asked, "How does the media impact the evolution of the industry?" He answered, "It's part of it, and it's always been part of it— and it's a little more out there now. I've taken the approach that I'm doing what I do, and whatever happens, happens. It's become so big." For the most part, the restaurant received good to excellent reviews. People liked the food. He stated his biggest challenge to be the diners:

"The diners are so educated now—and that's a great thing, but it's hard to do what you do because of their expectations. You have to become really, really conscious, and that can be overwhelming."

—CHEF MICHAEL CITARELLA

So, it's really interesting to be on this side, writing this book educating you on how to be more educated.

He told me recently that so many people are trying to make money from a story. Mike said, "There needs to be a little

---

224 Laura Shunk, "Reappearing Act: Michael Citarella's Journey to the Kitchen at the Monarch Room," *The Village Voice*, July 15, 2014.

bit of flare but now the writers are taking away from the substance. People are too busy looking for the story. They are missing everything else." If too many people continue to write about it, it takes away the magic of food and dining. For instance, farms have been around for millennia. They aren't new. People like me are continuing to talk about the farm-to-table aspect of dining. Mike, as a chef, doesn't need it to be about the source; it should be about the taste. He wants his guests to have their own experience—hopefully one that is enjoyed—so he makes the food and then backs off. Because of the challenges with educated diners, he *will* add the sources of his produce and meat to his menu. But he warns me. He has known chefs to claim ethical sources of meat on their menus when they are serving something other than that. No wonder my older brother holds a cynical view toward similar claims; you want to trust it to be true, but can you really?

AT THE RESTAURANT/MARKET

I am not trying to take away from the magic of dining out. If any of you know me, you know I'm far from obnoxious when it comes to ordering at restaurants. But, I am educating you and want you to own the source. So here's the dilemma: Since so much of what surrounds us is subjective, what if you were given two roasted chicken dinners, cooked exactly the same, except one is sourced from Bell & Evans and the other from Tyson? Whose responsibility is it to make that plate of food delicious—the chicken producer's or the chef's? Would you be able to taste the difference?

- Bell & Evans focuses on humane treatment: Chickens are raised without antibiotics and chicks are given immediate access to organic feed and water and are never handled by machinery.[225]
- Tyson does the opposite.

But does it really matter? Yes. The chef wants you to like the food. Dan Barber states, "Process trumps product."[226] If both plates are delicious, then the major bonus would be that you're eating "humanely" raised meat. If it makes you feel better, subjectively, and if your opinion is one that supports spending the extra money on the Bell & Evans chicken, that is your choice. This is about you knowing your options and choosing the restaurants that a) are transparent in their sourcing (with you trusting that it's true) and b) source ethically, locally, and sustainably in the first place. Per Humane Farm Animal Care's frequently asked questions:[227]

"If we can't persuade you to care about the treatment of farm animals on its own merits, then please know that raising a farm animal more humanely has a direct impact on your health and the health of the environment. Farm animals that are not raised humanely are fed diets of animal by-products, antibiotics and hormones. As far as the environment goes, fewer animals on more space is better for the land, the air, and the water."

---

225 "Our Standards," Bell & Evans, accessed May 4, 2020.

226 Dan Barber, *The Third Plate: Field Notes on the Future of Food* (New York: Penguin Books, 2015), 137.

227 "Frequently Asked Questions," Create a more humane world for farm animals, Certified Humane Raised & Handled, accessed May 4, 2020.

These are some names of ranches and farms that ethically raise animals. They are what to look for on menus—usually the fine print next to the dish or at the bottom—keeping in mind this isn't an exhaustive list. I could be missing your local/regional farm/ranch not listed on the ASPCA website encouraging us to eat/shop with our hearts:[228]

- **Chicken:** Bell & Evans, Ayrshire Farm, D'Artagnan, Firefly Farms, Joyce Farms, Mary's Free Range, Murray's, Sage Hill Farms, White Oak Pastures
- **Beef:** Ayrshire Farm, Baldwin Beef, Brasstown Beef, Crane Dance Farm, Firefly Farms, Hilltop Angus Farms, Joyce Farms, Mariposa Ranch, Niman Ranch, Redger Farms, Skagit River Ranch, Starwalker Organic Farms, Teton Waters Ranch, White Oak Pastures
- **Pork:** Archway Farm, Ayrshire Farm, Crane Dance Farm, Firefly Farms, Fra' Mani, Goodnight Brothers, Home Place Pastures, Joyce Farms, La Quercia, Llano Seco, Newman Farms, Niman Ranch, Starwalker Organic Farms, Thompson Farms, White Oak Pastures
- **Turkey:** Firefly Farms, Koch's Turkey, Mary's Free Range, Murray's, Sage Hill Farms, White Oak Pastures
- **Lamb:** Anderson Ranches, Central Grazing Company, Niman Ranch, Sun Raised Foods, White Oak Pastures
- **Bison:** Straight Arrow Bison
- **Seafood:** The ASPCA lists nothing for humanely raised seafood. So, instead, use the Monterey Bay Aquarium's

---

228 "Shop With Your Heart Brand List," Creating a More Humane World for Farm Animals, Consumer Resources, ASPCA, accessed May 4, 2020.

sustainable seafood watch. There is the national guide, the West Coast guide, and the sushi guide. You can download and print at www.seafoodwatch.org. The color-coded guides detail[229]:

- **Best Choices—green**
  Buy first; they're well managed and caught or farmed responsibly.
- **Good Alternatives—yellow**
  Buy, but be aware there are concerns with how they're caught, farmed, or managed.
- **Avoid—red**
  Take a pass on these for now; they're overfished, lack strong management, or are caught or farmed in ways that harm other marine life or the environment.

YOUR FAVORITE MEAL

Your favorite meal is waiting to be eaten, either at home or in the restaurant.

- You now have the power to be the best food sleuth possible.
- You know how to blast past labels, not to be intimidated at the farm stand or farmers market, and what to buy organic (shopping for all organic items is not bad; it's just that most people cannot afford it).
- You know that the health of the soil is imperative to your health.
- You have "met" the trailblazers who have led the way with this niche food education and who continue to use their resources to find people devoting their lives to being

---

229 "Consumer Guides," Monterey Bay Aquarium Seafood Watch, accessed May 4, 2020.

stewards of the land and water for the sake of the environment and the future of this earth.

Regenerative agriculture and holistic rotational grazing are important practices to feed the soil, manage water retention, reduce greenhouse gas emissions, and turn a profit. The favorite meal is one of love, taste, family, tradition, health, celebration and season. Eating seasonally is healthier because the products have not been treated with shelf life preservatives and the nutrients are in tip-top shape. You know how to talk to your farmer or vendor and ask questions if you are unfamiliar with a product—even better, ask them their favorite recipe and go back to let them know how it turned out. The beef and meat alternative industries are doing their best to be transparent in terms of sustainability and safety, but numerous processes are in place to get product to the consumer that are worth being mindful about.

We are all stakeholders as citizens of this Earth, having descended from the hominins. We have strayed so far from traditional ways of eating due to the industrial and agricultural revolutions, engineering faster and faster ways of living and eating. This is now even more evident during a pandemic. COVID-19 affected how we looked at food, down to what we valued and what was available. My thought is that you've become more creative and less afraid of different ingredients, using more local seasonal ingredients because they were abundant during the crisis. My heart goes out to the employees and families of the mega farms and meat industry as they continue to navigate business with new safety procedures.

I hope I have helped you discover the story behind your favorite meal and that you understand the relevance as you care about the quality of its source. I hope you have learned to care about nutrition while learning about the ethics of how the main components of your meal are produced. I hope choosing organic, or not, is less complicated or confusing. I hope you understand the impact of your choices as you circle back to the moral of the story: your favorite meal, so you can now tell your own stories.

Continue to be adventurous. Feel empowered to make good choices. Enjoy making and eating your favorite meal from start to finish, knowing its journey from the soil to your plate.

APPENDIX

___

INTRODUCTION

Farm Progress. "Average age of US farmer climbs to 57.5 years." April 11, 2019. *https://www.farmprogress.com/farm-life/average-age-us-farmer-climbs-575-years*

Howitt, Peter, dir. *Sliding Doors*. 1998; Los Angeles, CA: Miramax Films, Intermedia Films, Mirage Enterprises, Paramount Pictures. Film.

Row 7 Seed Company. "Our Story." Accessed May 18, 2020. *https://www.row7seeds.com/pages/our-story*.

Sincero, Jen. *You are a Badass: How to Stop Doubting Your Greatness and Start Living an Awesome Life*. Philadelphia: Running Press, 2013.

Team, The SOFA, and Cheryl Doss. "The role of women in agriculture." ESA Working Paper No. 11-02 (March 2011): 1-46.

World Food Programme. "Hunger Map 2019." August 14, 2019. *https://www.wfp.org/publications/2019-hunger-map*.

CHAPTER 1

Agricultural Marketing Service. "USDA Announces Additional Food Purchase Plans." May 4, 2020. *https://www.ams.usda.gov/press-release/usda-announces-additional-food-purchase-plans.*

Agricultural Marketing Service. "USDA Farmers to Families Food Box." Accessed May 31, 2020. *https://www.ams.usda.gov/selling-food-to-usda/farmers-to-families-food-box.*

Cameron, James, dir. *Avatar.* 2009; Los Angeles, CA: Twentieth Century Fox. Film.

Centers for Disease Control and Prevention. "Diabetes in the United States—A Snapshot." Accessed May 19, 2020. *https://www.cdc.gov/diabetes/library/socialmedia/infographics.html.*

Centers for Disease Control and Prevention. "Frequently Asked Questions." Coronavirus Disease 2019 (COVID-19). Updated June 2, 2020. *https://www.cdc.gov/coronavirus/2019-ncov/faq.html.*

Chai, Anna, Nari Kye, dirs. *Wasted! The Story of Food Waste.* 2017; New York, NY: Zero Point Zero. Documentary, 85 min.

Crowe, Cameron, dir. *Jerry Maguire.* 1996; Culver City, CA: TriStar Pictures. Film.

Cutforth, Dan, Jane Lipsitz, pros. *Top Chef Kentucky,* Episode 3, Naughty and Nice." Aired December 20, 2018, on Bravo.

Farm Progress. "Average age of US farmer climbs to 57.5 years." April 11, 2019. *https://www.farmprogress.com/farm-life/average-age-us-farmer-climbs-575-years*

Food and Agriculture Organization of the United Nations. "Food Loss and Food Waste." Accessed May 19, 2020. *http://www.fao.org/food-loss-and-food-waste/en/.*

Food and Agriculture Organization of the United Nations. "Food wastage footprint—Impacts on natural resources." Summary Report 2013. Accessed May 19, 2020. *http://www.fao.org/3/i3347e/i3347e.pdf.*

Food and Agriculture Organization of the United Nations. "Major cuts of greenhouse gas emissions from livestock within reach." September 26, 2013. *http://www.fao.org/news/story/en/item/197608/icode/.*

Food and Agriculture Organization of the United Nations. "Soils are endangered, but the degradation can be rolled back." December 4, 2015. *http://www.fao.org/news/story/en/item/357059/icode/.*

Gunders, Dana. "Wasted: How America Is Losing Up to 40 Percent of Its Food from Farm to Fork to Landfill?" NRDC. August 16, 2017. *https://www.nrdc.org/resources/wasted-how-america-losing-40-percent-its-food-farm-fork-landfill.*

Imperfect Foods. Accessed May 19, 2020. *https://www.imperfectfoods.com.*

Kroger. "Kroger Launches Expanded Dairy Rescue Program to Support Children and Families During COVID-19." Press Release. April 30, 2020. *http://ir.kroger.com/file/Index?KeyFile=403809933.*

Misfits Market. Accessed May 19, 2020. *https://www.misfitsmarket.com.*

Nuwer, Rachel. "Raising Beef Uses Ten Times More Resources than Poultry, Dairy, Eggs or Pork." *Smithsonian Magazine*, July 21, 2014. *https://www.smithsonianmag.com/science-nature/beef-uses-ten-times-more-resources-poultry-dairy-eggs-pork-180952103/.*

O'Hare, James. "2 Billion People Lack Proper Vitamins & Minerals—But This Group Wants to Change That." *Global Citizen,* March 29, 2017, *https://www.globalcitizen.org/en/content/harvestplus-hidden-hunger-biofortification-malnutr/.*

Price, Sterling. "Average Household Cost of Food." ValuePenguin by lendingtree. Accessed May 19, 2020. *https://www.valuepenguin.com/how-much-we-spend-food.*

Stabiner, Karen, Dan Barber. "Nearly a third of small, independent farmers are facing bankruptcy by the end of 2020, new survey says." *The Counter,* May 18, 2020, *https://thecounter.org/covid-19-dan-barber-resourced-small-farmer-survey/.*

Trader Joe's. "Our Story." Accessed May 18, 2020. *https://www.traderjoes.com/our-story.*

Trader Joe's. "2019 Sustainability Progress." Announcements, Sustainability. Accessed May 28, 2020. *https://www.traderjoes.com/announcement/2019-sustainability-progress.*

United Nations Environment Programme. *Why do we need to change our food system?* May 9, 2016. YouTube video, 3:46. *https://www.youtube.com/watch?v=VcL3BQeteCc.*

United Nations. "Growing at a slower pace, world population is expected to reach 9.7 billion in 2050 and could peak at nearly 11 billion around 2100." June 17, 2019. *https://www.un.org/development/desa/en/news/population/world-population-prospects-2019.html.*

US Food & Drug Administration. "Are You Storing Food Safely?" Accessed May 29, 2020. *https://www.fda.gov/consumers/consumer-updates/are-you-storing-food-safely.*

World Food Programme. "Hunger Statistics." Accessed May 29, 2020. *https://www.foodaidfoundation.org/world-hunger-statistics.html.*

World Health Organization. "Malnutrition is a world health crisis." Accessed May 19, 2020. *https://www.who.int/nutrition/topics/world-food-day-2019-malnutrition-world-health-crisis/en/.*

CHAPTER 2

Bali, Niti. *Farm to Fork Riot.* White River Junction: Chelsea Green, 2019.

Barber, Dan. "A foie gras parable." Filmed July 2008 in Napa, CA. Taste 3 Conference. TED Video, 20:25. *https://www.youtube.com/watch?v=gvrgDomAFoU.*

Barber, Dan. "How I fell in love with a fish." Filmed February 2010 in Long Beach, CA. TED video, 19:31. *https://www.youtube.com/watch?v=4EUAMe2ixCI.*

Barber, Dan. "The Chef's Role in the Creation of a Sustainable, Healthy Diet." Filmed November 2014 in Pocantico Hills, NY. 2014 Food for Tomorrow Conference. YouTube video, 24:26. *https://www.youtube.com/watch?v=ZQwn69A3z9A&t=295s.*

Barber, Dan. *The Third Plate: Field Notes on the Future of Food.* New York: Penguin Books, 2015.

Bull, Peter, Alex Gibney, Ryan Miller, and Caroline Suh, dirs. *Cooked.* 2016; New York, NY: Jigsaw Productions, Netflix. Documentary.

Encyclopaedia Britannica Online. Academic ed., s.v. "Foie Gras." Accessed May 17, 2020. *https://www.britannica.com/topic/foie-gras.*

Hodgkins, Martha, ed. *Letters to a Young Farmer: On Food, Farming, and Our Future.* New York: Princeton Architectural Press, 2017.

Kenner, Robert, dir. *Food, Inc.* 2008; New York, NY: Magnolia Pictures, Participant, River Road Entertainment. Documentary.

Pollan, Michael. *Cooked: A Natural History of Transformation.* New York: Penguin Press, 2013.

Pollan, Michael. *In Defense of Food: An Eater's Manifesto.* New York: Penguin Press, 2008.

Pollan, Michael. *Second Nature: A Gardener's Education.* New York: Grove Press, 1991.

Pollan, Michael. *The Omnivore's Dilemma.* New York: Penguin Press, 2006.

Riverside, University of California. "America's most widely consumed oil causes genetic changes in the brain: Soybean oil linked to metabolic and neurological changes in mice." ScienceDaily. January 17, 2020. *https://www.sciencedaily.com/releases/2020/01/200117080827.htm.*

Row 7 Seed Company. "Our Story." Accessed May 18, 2020. *https://www.row7seeds.com/pages/our-story.*

Salatin, Joel. *Everything I Want to Do is Illegal—War Stories from the Local Food Front.* Swoope: Polyface, Inc., 2007.

Salatin, Joel. *Holy Cows & Hog Heaven: The Food Buyer's Guide to Farm Friendly Food.* Swoope: Polyface, Inc., 2004.

Salatin, Joel. *Salad Bar Beef.* Swoope: Polyface, Inc., 1995.

Salatin, Joel. "Stomping Out," *Musings from the Lunatic Farmer* (blog), October 4, 2019. *https://www.thelunaticfarmer.com/blog/10/4/2019/stomping-out.*

Schwarz, Michael, dir. *Botany of Desire.* 2009; Menlo Park, CA: Kikim Media. Documentary.

Schwarz, Michael, dir. *In Defense of Food.* 2015; Menlo Park, CA: Kikim Media. Documentary.

CHAPTER 3

Berry, Wendell. *Bringing It to the Table: On Farming and Food.* Berkeley: Counterpoint, 2009.

Crowe, Cameron, dir. *Jerry Maguire.* 1996; Culver City, CA: TriStar Pictures. Film.

Pollan, Michael. "Michael Pollan's Ideal Meal." Interview by University of Minnesota Baaken Center for Spirituality & Healing, *Taking Charge of Your Health & Wellbeing,* YouTube, April 10, 2018. Video, 2:58. *https://www.youtube.com/watch?v=IdoUvo-Jd2rE&t=58s.*

Stanton, Andrew, dir. *WALL-E.* 2008; Burbank, CA: Walt Disney Pictures, Pixar, FortyFour Studios. Film.

The Food Industry Association. "Supermarket Facts." Accessed June 1, 2020. *https://www.fmi.org/our-research/supermarket-facts.*

Walters, Terry. *Clean Food: A Seasonal Guide to Eating Close to the Source.* New York: Sterling Epicure, revised & expanded 2012.

CHAPTER 4

Agricultural Marketing Service. "Introduction to Organic Practices." last modified September 2015. *https://www.ams.usda.gov/publications/content/introduction-organic-practices.*

Agricultural Marketing Service. "Pesticide Data Program." Accessed May 26, 2020. *https://www.ams.usda.gov/datasets/pdp.*

Agricultural Marketing Service. "The National List." Accessed June 1, 2020. *https://www.ams.usda.gov/rules-regulations/organic/national-list.*

Aldrich, Robert, dir. *The Dirty Dozen.* 1967; Beverly Hills, CA: Metro-Goldwyn-Mayer Studios Inc. Film.

Barański, Marcin, Dominika Srednicka-Tober, and Nickolaos Volakakis et al. "Higher Antioxidant and Lower Cadmium Concentrations and Lower Incidence of Pesticide Residues in Organically Grown Crops: A Systematic Literature Review and Meta-Analyses." *British Journal of Nutrition* 112, no. 5 (July 2015): 794-811. doi:10.1017/S0007114514001366

Cosmic Crisp. "Cosmic Crisp Story." Flavor. Accessed May 26, 2020. *https://cosmiccrisp.com/cosmic-crisp-story/.*

Cosmic Crisp. "Where to Buy Apples." Learn. Accessed May 26, 2020. *https://cosmiccrisp.com/where-to-buy-apples/.*

DeWeese, Adrianne. "Stephenson's old location to become Quik-Trip." *The Examiner,* June 29, 2011. *https://www.examiner.net/x177096941/Stephensons-old-location-to-become-QuikTrip.*

Environmental Working Group. "Clean Fifteen." EWG's 2020 Shopper's Guide to Pesticides in Produceä. Accessed May 26, 2020. *https://www.ewg.org/foodnews/clean-fifteen.php.*

Environmental Working Group. "Dirty Dozen." EWG's 2020 Shopper's Guide to Pesticides in Produceä. Accessed May 26, 2020. *https://www.ewg.org/foodnews/dirty-dozen.php.*

Environmental Working Group. "EWG's 2019 Shopper's Guide to Pesticides in Produceä." Accessed February 16, 2020. Link discontinued.

Environmental Working Group. "Should we eat more fruits and vegetables? What about the pesticide residue?" Frequently Asked Questions about Produce and Pesticides. Accessed May 26, 2020. *https://www.ewg.org/foodnews/faq.php#question-1.*

Fey, Tina, creator. "Liz Lemon." *30 Rock.* 2006-2013; New York, NY: National Broadcasting Company. Television series.

Hale Groves. "What is the difference between Navel Oranges and Cara Cara Oranges?" Fruit facts. September 4, 2018. *https://www.halegroves.com/blog/what-is-the-difference-between-navel-oranges-and-cara-cara-oranges/.*

Langlois, Maureen. "Organic Pesticides: Not An Oxymoron." *Shots, Health News from NPR.* NPR, June 17, 2011. *https://www.npr.org/sections/health-shots/2011/06/18/137249264/organic-pesticides-not-an-oxymoron.*

McNeil, Maggie. "US organic sales break through $50 billion mark in 2018." Press Release. Organic Trade Association. May 17, 2019. *https://ota.com/news/press-releases/20699.*

Merriam-Webster. s.v. "Organic." Accessed May 26, 2020. *https://www.merriam-webster.com/dictionary/organic*

Mie, Axel, Helle Raun Andersen, Stefan Gunnarsson, Johannes Kahl, Emmanuelle Kesse-Guyot, Ewa Rembialkowska, Gianluca Quaglio, Philippe Grandjean. "Human health implications of organic food and organic agriculture: a comprehensive review." *Environmental health: a global access science source* 16, no.1 (October 2017): 111. doi:10.1186/s12940-017-0315-4

National Agricultural Library. "Organic Production/Organic Food: Information Access Tools." Accessed May 17, 2020. *https://www. nal.usda.gov/afsic/organic-productionorganic-food-information-access-tools.*

Oregon Tilth. "Transforming Farming and Food: Through Sustainable and Rigorous Standards." Certification. Accessed June 2, 2020. *https://tilth.org/certification/.*

United States Department of Agriculture. "Certifier Locator," Organic Integrity Database. Accessed June 2, 2020. *https:// organic.ams.usda.gov/integrity/Certifiers/CertifiersLocations-SearchPage.aspx.*

USDA Organic. "What is Organic Certification?" Last modified June 2012. *https://www.ams.usda.gov/sites/default/files/media/ What%20is%20Organic%20Certification.pdf.*

United States Environmental Protection Agency. "Food and Pesticides." Accessed May 26, 2020. *https://www.epa.gov/safepest-control/food-and-pesticides.*

CHAPTER 5

Addison, Keith. "Albert Howard." Journey to Forever. Accessed May 17, 2020. *http://journeytoforever.org/farm_library/howard. html.*

Berry, Wendell. *Bringing It to the Table: On Farming and Food.* Berkeley: Counterpoint, 2009.

Brown, Gabe. "Keys to Building a Healthy Soil." *Holistic Regeneration of Our Lands: A Producer's Perspective,"* Idaho Center for Sustainable Agriculture's annual symposium. Filmed November 28, 2014 by Transcend Productions in Boise, ID. YouTube video, 58:52. *https://www.youtube.com/watch?v=9yPjoh9YJMk.*

carbon nation. "Soil Carbon." Accessed October 7, 2019. *https://www.carbonnationmovie.com/soil-carbon.*

Chester, John, dir. *The Biggest Little Farm.* 2018; Los Angeles, CA: Diamond Docs, FarmLore Films. Documentary.

Davis, Donald R., Melvin Epp, and Hugh D. Riordan. "Changes in USDA Food Composition for 43 Garden Crops, 1950-1999." *Journal of the American College of Nutrition* 23, no. 6 (May 2004): 669-682. doi:10.1080/07315724.2004.10719409.

Grass Fed Solutions. "Soil Carbon Cowboys." Accessed October 7, 2019. *https://www.grass-fed-solutions.com/carbon.html.*

History. "Dust bowl." Updated February 21, 2020. *https://www.history.com/topics/great-depression/dust-bowl.*

Howard, Sir Albert. *An Agricultural Testament.* New York: Oxford University Press, 1943.

Intergovernmental Panel on Climate Change. "Desertification." Special Report: Special Report on Climate Change and Land. Accessed May 21, 2020. *https://www.ipcc.ch/srccl/chapter/chapter-3/.*

Joyce Farms. "Dr. Allen Williams, Ph.D." Accessed May 21, 2020. *https://joyce-farms.com/pages/dr-allen-williams.*

Merriam-Webster. s.v. "dead zone." Accessed May 21, 2020. *https://www.merriam-webster.com/dictionary/dead%20zone.*

Peters, May, Suchada Langley, and Paul Westcott. "Agricultural Commodity Prices Spikes in the 1970s and 1990s: Valuable Lessons for Today." Economic Research Service, USDA. March 1, 2009. *https://www.ers.usda.gov/amber-waves/2009/march/*

agricultural-commodity-price-spikes-in-the-1970s-and-1990s-valuable-lessons-for-today/.

Roosevelt, Franklin Delano. Fireside Chat on Drought Conditions. September 9, 1936. Retrieved from the Digital Public Library of America. Accessed January 19, 2020. *http://catalog.archives.gov/id/197309*

Savory, Allan. "How Livestock and Grassland Soils Can Save Civilization." Northern Plains Grasslands Symposium. Filmed July 19, 2017 in Bismarck, ND. YouTube video, 1:48:54. *https://www.youtube.com/watch?v=wHzA9wob7io&t=8s.*

Savory Institute. "Our Mission." About us. Accessed May 21, 2020. *https://savory.global/our-mission/.*

Scheer, Roddy, Doug Moss. "Dirt Poor: Have Fruits and Vegetables Become Less Nutritious?" EarthTalk. *Scientific American,* April 27, 2011. *https://www.scientificamerican.com/article/soil-depletion-and-nutrition-loss/.*

Thompson, Anne. "Why Breakout Documentary 'The Biggest Little Farm' Didn't Sell to Netflix, from Poop to Nuts." IndieWire. May 13, 2019. *https://www.indiewire.com/2019/05/the-biggest-little-farm-documentary-breakout-1202139364/.*

United States Environmental Protection Agency. "The Effects: Environment." Nutrient pollution. Accessed May 21, 2020. *https://www.epa.gov/nutrientpollution/effects-environment.*

US Food & Drug Administration. "Outbreak Investigation of E. coli: Romaine from Salinas, California (November 2019)." May 21, 2020. *https://www.fda.gov/food/outbreaks-foodborne-illness/outbreak-investigation-e-coli-romaine-salinas-california-november-2019.*

Williams, Allen. "Allen Williams—Restore Soil and Ecosystem Health with Adaptive Grazing." Quiriva Conference, *Ranching and Farming at the Radical Center.* Filmed by Crash Roll Films in Albuquerque, NM., November 15-17, 2017. YouTube video, 42:30. *https://www.youtube.com/watch?v=BwH6od6Jaq8.*

Woolner, David. "FDR and the New Deal Response to an Environmental Catastrophe." *Energy & Environment, Franklin & Eleanor* (blog). *Roosevelt Institute,* June 3, 2010. *https://rooseveltinstitute.org/fdr-and-new-deal-response-environmental-catastrophe/.*

CHAPTER 6

AnimalClock "Annual US Animal Death Stats." 2020 US Animal Kill Clock. *Humane Ventures.* Accessed June 3, 2020. *https://animalclock.org.*

Animal Legal & Historical Center. "Humane Slaughter Act." United States Code Annotated, Title 7, Agriculture, Chapter 48. Humane Methods of Livestock Slaughter. Michigan State University. Last checked February 2020. *https://www.animallaw.info/statute/us-food-animal-humane-methods-livestock-slaughter.*

Bruett, Cameron. "Defining Sustainability for the Cattle Industry." Texoma Cattlemen's Conference. Filmed March 21, 2015 in Ardmore, OK. YouTube video, 57:38. *https://www.youtube.com/watch?v=P1dxuX4glqc&t=429s.*

Cargill. "Meat & Poultry." Products & Services. Accessed May 17, 2020. *https://www.cargill.com/meat-poultry.*

Davis, University of California-. "Kimberly Stackhouse-Lawson." 2018 Award of Distinction Recipients. College of Agricultural and Environmental Sciences. Accessed June 3, 2020.

https://caes.ucdavis.edu/news/events/college-celebration/recipients/2018-award-of-distinction-recipients.

EarthSave. "Food Choices and the Planet." Healthy People Healthy Planet. Accessed May 26, 2020. http://www.earthsave.org/environment.htm.

Galasso, Philip E. "Pink slime is banned in Europe, it should be banned in the US" The Citizens' Voice. April 20, 2012. https://m.citizensvoice.com/opinion/letters/pink-slime-is-banned-in-europe-it-should-be-banned-in-the-u-s-1.1307028.

Global Roundtable for Sustainable Beefâ. "What is Sustainable Beef?" Accessed October 24, 2019. https://grsbeef.org/WhatIs-SustainableBeef.

Grandin, Temple. "Interpretation of the North American Meat Institute (NAMI) Animal Handling Guidelines for auditing the welfare of cattle, pigs, and sheep at slaughter plants." Grandin. Updated January 2020. https://www.grandin.com/interpreting.ami.guidelines.html.

Grandin, Temple. "Recommended Animal Handling Guidelines & Audit Guide: A Systematic Approach to Animal Welfare." Animal Handling. North American Meat Institute. July 24, 2013.

Green, Joel L. "Lean Finely Textured Beef: The 'Pink Slime' Controversy." Congressional Research Service. April 6, 2012. https://www.foodpoisonjournal.com/uploads/image/R42473.pdf.

Gunnars, Kris. "Grass-Fed vs. Grain-fed Beef—What's the Difference?" Healthline. December 4, 2019. https://www.healthline.com/nutrition/grass-fed-vs-grain-fed-beef.

Hagen, Elisabeth. "Setting the Record Straight on Beef." *Health and Safety* (blog), US Department of Agriculture. February

21, 2017. *https://www.usda.gov/media/blog/2012/03/22/setting-record-straight-beef.*

Harrison, Carol. "Grass-fed or grain-fed beef, what's healthier?" Think Beef. February 28, 2019. *https://thinkbeef.ca/grass-fed-or-grain-fed-beef-whats-healthier/.*

JBS USA. "Animal Care." 2019 Key Facts and Figures. Accessed May 17, 2020. *https://sustainability.jbssa.com/chapters/animal-care/.*

JBS USA. "Cameron Bruett." JBS USA Leadership. Accessed October 24, 2019. *https://jbssa.com/about/leadership/.*

JBS USA. "Kimberly Stackhouse-Lawson." Who We Are. Our Sustainability Team. Accessed June 3, 2020. *https://sustainability.jbssa.com/chapters/who-we-are/.*

National Beef. "Quality, Value and Service." Accessed May 17, 2020. *https://www.nationalbeef.com/about-us/we-know-beef/focused-on-success.*

National Cattlemen's Beef Association. "Industry Statistics." Beef Industry Overview. Accessed June 3, 2020. *https://www.ncba.org/beefindustrystatistics.aspx.*

National Hog Farmer. "NAMI: Working trade agreements with Japan, South Korea crucial." US Meat Export Federation. April 30, 2019. *https://www.nationalhogfarmer.com/agenda/nami-working-trade-agreements-japan-south-korea-crucial*

Nestle, Marion. "Meat: the ongoing saga." *Food Politics* (blog). June 3, 2020. *https://www.foodpolitics.com/2020/06/meat-the-ongoing-saga/.*

North American Meat Institute. "Sodium Nitrite: The Facts." November 2008. *https://www.meatinstitute.org/index.php?ht=a/GetDocumentAction/i/44170.*

Potts, Julie Anna. North Carolina Farm Bureau Federation's Annual Meeting 2014. Filmed December 2014 in Greensboro, NC. YouTube video, 18:57. *https://www.youtube.com/watch?v=2mozMvYS1RQ.*

Psihoyos, Louie, dir. *Gamechangers.* 2018; ReFuel Productions, Oceanic Preservation Society, Diamond Docs. Documentary.

Robbins, Ocean. "The Surprising Truth About Antibiotics, Factory Farms, and Food Recalls." Food Revolution Network. January 18, 2019. *https://foodrevolution.org/blog/antibiotic-resistance-factory-farms/.*

Rutherford, Burt. "Industry Embarks On First Sustainability Study." *Beef Magazine.* February 21, 2013. *https://www.beefmagazine.com/management/industry-embarks-first-sustainability-study.*

Rutherford, Burt. "Is sustainability sustainable?" *Beef Editor's Blog* (blog). *Beef Magazine.* March 8, 2017. *https://www.beefmagazine.com/ranching/sustainability-sustainable.*

Stackhouse-Lawson, Kim. "Beef Checkoff Program Sustainability Research." Texoma Cattlemen's Conference. Filmed March 21, 2015 in Ardmore, OK, YouTube video, 39:26. *https://www.youtube.com/watch?v=2MR4ymCYnTI&t=2068s.*

Tyson Foods. "Getting From Farm to Table." Accessed May 17, 2020. *https://www.tysonfoods.com/innovation/protein-leader/getting-farm-table.*

United States Department of Agriculture. "Quarterly Enforcement Report for Quarter 2, Fiscal Year 2020." Regulatory Compliance. Food Safety and Inspection Service. Accessed June 2, 2020. *https://www.fsis.usda.gov/wps/portal/fsis/topics/regulatory-compliance/regulatory-enforcement/quarterly-enforcement-reports/qer-q1-fy2020.*

US Food & Drug Administration. "Bovine Somatotropin (bST)." April 21, 2020. *https://www.fda.gov/animal-veterinary/product-safety-information/bovine-somatotropin-bst.*

US Food & Drug Administration. "Food Irradiation: What You Need to Know." January 4, 2018. *https://www.fda.gov/media/81259/download.*

Whole Foods Market. "Meat Department Quality Standards." Accessed April 27, 2020. *https://www.wholefoodsmarket.com/quality-standards/meat-standards.*

Yang, Jason. "How To Butcher An Entire Cow—Every Cut Of Meat Explained." *Handcrafted* from Bon Appetit Video. Released May 17, 2017. YouTube video, 18:47. *https://www.youtube.com/watch?v=WrOzwoMKzH4.*

CHAPTER 7

Beyond Meat®. "Find Us Near You." Restaurants & Stores. Accessed April 27, 2020. *https://www.beyondmeat.com/where-to-find/.*

Beyond Meat®. "Frequently Asked Questions." Beyond Burger®. Accessed April 27, 2020. *https://www.beyondmeat.com/faqs/.*

Beyond Meat®. "Our Ingredients." How we make meat from plants. Accessed April 27, 2020. *https://www.beyondmeat.com/about/our-ingredients/.*

Beyond Meat®. "Our Products." Beyond Burger. Accessed April 27, 2020. *https://www.beyondmeat.com/products/.*

Carl's Jr.® "Beyond Famous Star With Cheese." Menu & Nutrition. Accessed May 26, 2020. *https://fastfoodnutrition.org/carls-jr/beyond-famous-star-with-cheese.*

Eisen, Michael. "How GMOs can Save Civilization [Impossible Food]." Next Generation Nations™. Accessed May 26, 2020. *https://ngn.org/news/how-gmos-can-save-civilization-and-probably-already-have-impossible-food/.*

Heller, Martin C. and Gregory A. Keoleian, "Beyond Meat's Beyond Burger Life Cycle Assessment: A detailed comparison between a plant-based and an animal-based protein source." School for Environment & Sustainability. University of Michigan. *Center for Sustainable Systems.* No. CSS18-10. September 14, 2018. *http://css.umich.edu/publication/beyond-meats-beyond-burger-life-cycle-assessment-detailed-comparison-between-plant-based.*

Hiruma, Toshiuki, Ray Jafelice, Dave Cox, Ken Stephenson, and Edouard David, dirs. *Inspector Gadget.* Beverly Hills, CA: DIC Enterprises, 1983-1986. Television cartoon series.

Impossible™ Foods. "How Do You Make Heme?" Frequently Asked Questions. Accessed April 27, 2020. *https://faq.impossiblefoods.com/hc/en-us/articles/360034767354-How-do-you-make-heme-.*

Impossible™ Foods. "Impossible At Home." Now available in select grocery stores. Accessed April 27, 2020. *https://impossiblefoods.com/locations/.*

Impossible™ Foods. "What Are The Ingredients?" Frequently Asked Questions. Accessed April 27, 2020. *https://faq.impossiblefoods.com/hc/en-us/articles/360018937494-What-are-the-ingredients-.*

Impossible™ Foods. "What is Soy Leghemoglobin, or Heme?" Frequently Asked Questions. Accessed April 27, 2020. *https://faq.impossiblefoods.com/hc/en-us/articles/360019100553-What-is-soy-leghemoglobin-or-heme-.*

Khan, Sofia, Jon Dettling, Cristobal Loyola, Joshua Hester, and Rebekah Moses. "Environmental Life Cycle Analysis: Impossible Burger 2.0." Executive Summary. Impossible Foods. March 2019. *https://impossiblefoods.com/mission/lca-update-2019/.*

McDonalds. "P.L.T." Plant. Lettuce. Tomato. Accessed June 3, 2020. *https://www.mcdonalds.com/ca/en-ca/local/plt.html.*

Mitroff, Sarah. "The ultimate Impossible Burger vs Beyond Meat Burger taste test." Healthy Eating. Health and Wellness. CNET. September 20, 2019. *https://www.cnet.com/health/impossible-burger-vs-beyond-meat-burger-our-ultimate-taste-test/*

Silverman, Hollie. "A vegan man claims Burger King cooked Impossible Whopper alongside meat." CNN Business. Updated November 19, 2019. *https://www.cnn.com/2019/11/19/business/burger-king-impossible-burger-lawsuit-trnd/index.html.*

Strahler, Steven R. "Don Thompson's fake-meat fortune soars." Consumer products, Crain's Chicago Business. June 7, 2019. *https://www.chicagobusiness.com/consumer-products/don-thompsons-fake-meat-fortune-soars.*

U.N. Environment. "Champions of the Earth." Annual Report 2018. Accessed March 4, 2020. *https://www.unenvironment.org/annualreport/2018/index.php#ch-11.*

Yang, Royston. "Why Beyond Meat Soared 29% in May." Nasdaq. June 2, 2020. *https://www.nasdaq.com/articles/why-beyond-meat-soared-29-in-may-2020-06-03.*

CHAPTER 8

Cameron, James, dir. *Avatar.* 2009; Los Angeles, CA: Twentieth Century Fox. Film.

Colbin, Annemarie. *The Book of Whole Meals.* New York: Ballantine Books, 1983.

Cordain, Loren, S Boyd Eaton, Anthony Sebastian, Neil Mann, Staffan Lindeberg, Bruce A Watkins, James H O'Keefe, Janette Brand-Miller. "Origins and Evolution of the Western Diet: Health Implications for the 21st century." *The American Journal of Clinical Nutrition* 81, no. 2 (February 2005): 341-354. doi:10.1093/ajcn.81.2.341.

Merriam-Webster. s.v. "healthy." Accessed April 30, 2020. *https:// www.merriam-webster.com/dictionary/health*

Rohland, Tracy. "Fats, Carbs, and Protein: The Balancing Act." Down to Earth Organic & Natural. May 3, 2020. *https://www. downtoearth.org/health/nutrition/fats-carbs-and-protein-balancing-act*

Seasonal Food Guide. "Seasonal Food Guide." Find what's in season near you. Accessed April 27, 2020. *https://www.seasonalfoodguide.org.*

Turner, Kristina. *The Self-Healing Cookbook: Whole Foods to Balance Body, Mind & Moods.* Vashon Island: Earthtone Press, 2002.

CHAPTER 9

American Diabetes Association. "Navigating Nutrient Claims." Understanding Food Labels. Accessed May 3, 2020. *https:// www.diabetes.org/nutrition/understanding-food-labels/nutrient-content.*

American Diabetes Association. "What Can I Eat?" Nutrition Overview. Accessed July 18, 2019. *https://www.diabetes.org/ blog/what-can-i-eat.*

American Heart Association. "Heart-Check in the Grocery Store." Company Collaboration. Accessed May 3, 2020. *https://www. heart.org/en/healthy-living/healthy-eating/heart-check-foods.*

American Heart Association, "How a Food Becomes Heart-Check Certified." Company Collaboration. Accessed May 3, 2020. *https://www.heart.org/en/healthy-living/company-collaboration/heart-check-certification/how-a-food-becomes-heart-check-certified.*

Costello, Elvis. *Watching the Detectives.* Stiff Records (UK). Released October 1977.

Hargitay, Mariska. "Captain Olivia Benson." *Law & Order Special Victims Unit.* Created by Dick Wolf. New York, NY: NBC Studios, 1999-2020. Television series.

Humane Animal Farm Care. "How to decode egg labels." Accessed May 3, 2020. *https://certifiedhumane.org/decode-egg-labels/.*

Mitchell, Alice. "Chicken Producers Don't Use Growth Hormones: Here are the Reasons Why." The Poultry Site. April 12, 2016. *https://thepoultrysite.com/articles/chicken-producers-dont-use-growth-hormones-here-are-the-reasons-why.*

Nestle, Marion. *Unsavory Truth: How Food Companies Skew the Science of What We Eat.* New York: Basic Books, 2018.

Nestle, Marion. *What To Eat.* New York: North Point Press, 2006.

Stampler, Laura. "The Bizarre History of Women's Clothing Sizes." *Time.* October 23, 2014. *https://time.com/3532014/women-clothing-sizes-history/*

Stuart, Mel, dir. Lyrics by Leslie Bricusse, and Anthony Newley. *Willy Wonka & the Chocolate Factory.* 1971; Hollywood, CA: Paramount Pictures. Film.

The Humane Society of the United States. "How to decipher egg carton labels." A guide to egg labels. Accessed May 3, 2020. *https://www.humanesociety.org/resources/how-decipher-egg-carton-labels.*

US Food & Drug Administration. "Food Serving Sizes Get a Reality Check." Food & Beverages. July 16, 2016. *https://www.fda.gov/consumers/consumer-updates/food-serving-sizes-get-reality-check.*

US Food & Drug Administration. "Questions and Answers on Health Claims in Food Labeling." Food Labeling & Nutrition. December 13, 2017. *https://www.fda.gov/food/food-labeling-nutrition.*

Williams, Richard, Michael L. Marlow, and Edward Archer. "Retrospective Analysis of the Regulations Implementing the Nutrition Labeling and Education Act of 1990."

Regulation, Mercatus Center, George Mason University. April 12, 2016. *https://www.mercatus.org/publications/regulation/retrospective-analysis-regulations-implementing-nutrition-labeling-and.*

CHAPTER 10

ASPCA. "Shop With Your Heart Brand List." Creating a More Humane World for Farm Animals. Consumer Resources. Accessed May 4, 2020. *https://www.aspca.org/shopwithyourheart/consumer-resources.*

Barber, Dan. *The Third Plate: Field Notes on the Future of Food.* New York: Penguin Books, 2015.

Bell & Evans. "Our Standards." Accessed May 4, 2020. *https://www.bellandevans.com/our-standards/.*

Humane Farm Animal Care. "Frequently Asked Questions." Accessed May 4, 2020. *https://certifiedhumane.org/how-we-work/frequently-asked-questions/.*

Monterey Bay Aquarium Seafood Watch. "Consumer Guides." Accessed May 4, 2020. *https://www.montereybayaquarium.org/ act-for-the-ocean/sustainable-seafood/what-you-can-do.*

Shunk, Laura. "Reappearing Act: Michael Citarella's Journey to the Kitchen at the Monarch Room." *The Village Voice,* July 15, 2014. *https://www.villagevoice.com/2014/07/15/reappearing-act-mi- chael-citarellas-journey-to-the-kitchen-at-the-monarch-room/.*

ACKNOWLEDGMENTS

———

I would be remiss to not thank my friend Kevin of cheesy garlic bread fame for *really* being the catalyst for this process. Jen Sincero, figuratively, gave me the nudge, but it was Kevin who suggested I seek out Creator Institute with Eric Koester, knowing I had things to say.

Along with Kevin, I need to acknowledge my other interviewees who opened up about their favorite meals and shared their time amidst busy schedules to start this conversation: Brooke, Heather, Bryan, David, Paul, Laura, and Mike. To Terry, Niti, Joel, Jamie, Brendan, and the others who answered my emails, thank you.

Leading the charge to get this off the ground was my team of 120 strong Indiegogo campaign supporters who financially backed this project, which I launched the *same week* that our country shut down due to COVID-19. Your positivity kept me going as I asked myself if this was the right time to be completing this book.

I have to specifically thank my past and present colleagues at Cottage Rehabilitation Hospital. You compose the majority of my supporters. Thank you! I admire the work you do every day to ensure the safety and well-being of our patients.

Also, Davis, Dad, Sharon, Chris, Gelen, Derek (1), Mandy, Steven, Briana & Christian, Michael & Caroline, Carol, Derek (2), Chernee, Sarah, Elizabeth, Danelle, Joanie, Domi, Jamie and Kelly: I owe you a debt of gratitude. This book could not have happened without you.

And, finally, my editing teams at Creator Institute and New Degree Press. You have made the process for first time authors as streamlined as possible. Thank you for your gentle pushes, expertise, kindness, and the grace for the occasional hyper-stressed-out verbal processing.

If you have found enjoyment going through this journey, please consider reviewing the book. Writing a review is one of the most powerful ways to promote growth while still maintaining integrity. I'd love for you to share your thoughts in order for future readers to understand the nuggets of this book and for me to keep striving for good.

Let's have a favorite meal together and find where we all fit into this multifaceted relationship with the land, water, and animals.

Thank you.
Laura Isham

Made in the USA
San Bernardino, CA
14 August 2020

77048707R00131